Foreword by Dr. Gordon

Dr. Bruce Cook

Partnering with the Prophetic

Portfolios, Protocols, Patterns & Processes

Study Guide Included

Third Edition February 2014.

PARTNERING WITH THE PROPHETIC
Printed in the USA.
ISBN: 978-1-9399441-7-7
Library of Congress Control Number: 2013952586

Cover Design & Interior Formatting: Wendy K. Walters

Published By

 **KINGDOM HOUSE** P U B L I S H I N G

LAKEBAY, WASHINGTON, USA

To Contact the Author:
w w w . K i n g d o m H o u s e . n e t
w w w . K E Y S n e t w o r k . o r g

Dedication

To the Kingdom Givers in my Life:

You understand the principles of giving and honor.
May the Lord increase and multiply your seed and tribe.

Dr. Gordon Bradshaw
Dr. Mark Kauffman
Caroline Cook
Lottie Mae Cook
John & Mary Anderson
Jon Grieser
Mike & Janet Rovner
Mark & Suzi Henderson
Christopher & Debbie James
Charlie & Lisa Fisher
James Nesbit
Jackie, Sandy & Albert Seeno Jr.
JoAn Risdon
Doug & Therese Wall
Eli & Sheryl Valenzuela
Todd & Wendy Walters
Ashley Wolfe
Alex McCaskill
Dr. Phil Ming Xu

"A generous man will prosper; he who
refreshes others will himself be refreshed."

Proverbs 25:11 *(NIV)*

Anyone who receives a prophet because he is a prophet will receive a prophet's reward, and anyone who receives a righteous man because he is a righteous man will receive a righteous man's reward.

Matthew 10:41 NIV

Recognition

I would like to recognize and thank a few special people who have made my work easier and my burden lighter in the process of writing this book, and/or helped to make this book possible. First, I thank my wife Caroline for her grace, love, patience, support and encouragement. Next, I thank my mother Lottie Cook for exposing me to Christianity as a child and encouraging my spiritual development and love of reading. Third, I honor my former pastors, Mark and Suzi Henderson, for their friendship, dedication, sacrifice and commitment to the local church, and their example and leadership in five-fold ministry and discipling. Fourth, I recognize Apostle Dr. Gordon E. Bradshaw, as a valuable resource and biblical scholar, friend, brother, orator, revelator, and prophetic role model. He and Apostle Henderson have researched many of the Greek and Hebrew terms for me. Fifth, I acknowledge Prophet Peggy Cole, who gave me my first prophecy in 1995 — one that has since come to pass. Sixth, I thank John Bibee, Martha Rasco, and Robin MacEwan, who were instrumental in my receiving the baptism of the Holy Spirit in January 1995. Seventh, I honor Prophet Jess Bielby, who called me out of a crowd in June 2002 and prophesied me into ministry and helped to launch me in the prophetic. Thank you Jess for helping to confirm my spiritual identity and gifting, and Mark for mentoring me.

Finally, I acknowledge and thank the prophets (and in some cases, apostle-prophets) who have influenced my life in addition to those already named—Dr. Bill Hamon, Dr. Rick Joyner, Patricia King, Marc Brisebois, Shawn Bolz, James Goll, Steve Schulz, Kim Clement, Bob Jones, Stacey Campbell, Kirk Bennett, Bob Hartley, Gary Beaton, Marc Dupont, Larry Randolph, Dr. Chuck Pierce, Michelle Seidler, Barbara Wentroble, David and Petie Newsome, Ras and Bev Robinson, Jill and Michael O'Brien, Graham Cooke, Keith and Janet Miller, Kris Valloton, Dr. Sharon Stone, Dr. Paula Price, Dr. Jimmie Reed, Dr. Richard Eberiga, Dr. Betty Evans, Dr. Raymond Larson, James and Margie Brewton, Paul Nesbitt, Curtis Gillespie, Randy Patterson, Keith and Jane Hinsz, Dr. Doug Atha, Lyn McClendon, Jayne Ferriss, Iain Speirs, Sherry Brown, Jane Jones, Dr. Stan Jeffery, John Schenck, Dr. Michelle Morrison, Charles and Liz Robinson, Dr. Emmanuel Ziga, Daniel Pringle, Carla Campos, Bob Long, Vance and Debbie Russell, David Gardiner, Anthony and Susan Hulsebus, Stephen and Julie Bundra, Mike and Cindy Jacobs, Mickey and Sandie Freed, Robyn Thom Rodgers, Tosh Sturgess, Chris Cole, Phyllis Ford, Chris Herzog, Brian Francis Hume, Frances Lloyd, David Shadbolt, Simon Okwayo, Benjamin Arde, Richard Darnell, James Nesbit, Joan Manley, Elizabeth Alves, Marcie Rivera, Dr. Bradley Stuart, Don Morrison, Cary Stultz, Dennis Wiedrick, Randy DeMain, Sharnael Wolverton, Gustav du Toit, Bobby Conner, Steve Thompson, Sharon Billins, Donald Lisle, John Anderson, Jon Grieser, Jackie Seeno, Jeff Kingshott, Sharyn Dacbert, Tim Taylor, David Regnier, Lloyd Phillips, Johnny Enlow, Timothy Snodgrass, Karla Shrake, Lora Allison, Dr. Kluane Spake, Nicki Pfeifer, David VanKoevering, Dr. Francis Myles, Dr. Arleen Westerhof, Paul Cuny, Wendy Walters, Duncan Campbell, Sheri Hohs, Dr. Gayle Rogers, Jane Hamon, Dr. Mark Kauffman, Dr. Lance Wallnau, Dr. Clyde Rivers, Dr. A.L. (Papa) Gill and others.

Contents

Surely the Lord GOD
does nothing, unless He
reveals His secret to His
servants the prophets.
Amos 3:7 NKJV

Endorsements

Partnering with the Prophetic is an excellent resource of information for those hungry to learn more about prophetic ministry in the Body of Christ. 1 Cor. 14:1 says, "Follow the way of love and eagerly desire spiritual gifts, especially the gift of prophecy" (NIV). Having the opportunity to witness the Lord working with Dr. Bruce Cook as the senior prophet in our local church setting for many years, I'm not sure that I know of anyone who more eagerly desires for the gift of prophecy to come forth and to mature than Bruce. Dr. Cook shares his valuable insights from many years of experience in learning how the prophetic giftings and offices successfully operate in many different settings, not just the local church. I highly recommend this book for those new to the prophetic, but also for all of us who have been used in various levels of the prophetic and desire to know more.

Mark Henderson
Senior Leader | Glory House Christian Center
www.gloryhouse.net
Austin, TX

It is an unfortunate fact that numbers of Christian leaders have decided to avoid prophets and prophetic ministry. There is actually no good reason for this. ***Partnering with the Prophetic*** has the potential to turn our sad state of affairs around! Bruce Cook, in a straightforward and lucent manner, shows decisively how authentic prophecy is designed by God to bring benefit and blessing to every individual and every group of believers both in the church and in the workplace.

Dr. C. Peter Wagner
Apostolic Ambassador | Global Spheres, Inc.
www.globalspheres.org
Colorado Springs, CO

Dr. Bruce Cook's book ***Partnering with the Prophetic*** is indeed a resource that every student or minister of the prophetic should have in their library. He skillfully teaches, instructs, and imparts faith for activation in this timely book. I have both witnessed the operation of Bruce Cook's prophetic gift and received prophetic blessing and encouragement from God through him. Both Bruce and his gift are authentic -- true gifts to the Body of Christ.

Patricia King
Author, Speaker, CEO, Co-Founder of XPmedia
www.xpmedia.com
Maricopa, AZ

Partnering with the Prophetic is a powerful kingdom tool for those who want to increase their understanding when partnering with the prophetic and execution of this gift. Jesus said, *"In the last days false Prophets will arise."*

Therefore, it is important that we know how to discern and accurately identify this gift and those who operate in it. Bruce Cook has a fresh insight as one learns to and/or partners with the prophetic.

Dr. Elizabeth (Beth) Alves
President | Increase International
www.increaseinternational.com
Bulverde, TX

Dr. Bruce Cook has blessed the Body of Christ with wisdom and insight concerning Prophets and Prophetic Ministry. Every Christian needs to read this book to become knowledgeable of principles and practices of true prophets and prophetic ministry.

Dr. Bill Hamon
Author, Speaker
Bishop | Christian International Ministries Network
www.cimn.net
Santa Rosa Beach, FL

It is my great pleasure and honor to endorse **Partnering with the Prophetic** by my good friend, Dr. Bruce Cook. I believe that this timely book was ordained by the Lord to activate and uncover those prophetic people whose hearts are truly positioned to move forward in the fullness of their calling. Secondly, I am pleased in the progress that Dr. Bruce Cook has made in his own prophetic walk. This book should help unveil a life whose dedication is to serve the Lord with all their heart. I pray that people will understand how Dr. Bruce Cook received a God-given word at the appointed time and with hunger and thirst pursued the Lord to embrace the purpose of his life and his destiny. This book should be an example and testimony of one man's ability to allow God to lead him. I pray that each and every person that reads this book would make the same decision. To God be the Glory.

Jess Bielby
President of Gospel Associates
President of Apostolic Council of Churches and Ministries
Founder of Kansas Food for Life
www.mygodlives.org | www.besthomefoods.com
Benton, KS

Dr. Bruce Cook has accomplished and completed this work, **Partnering with the Prophetic.** He continually surprises me with his many gifts and talents, and now as an author. I have observed how the Lord has added to his life and ministry, line upon line, and precept upon precept. On a personal level, Dr. Cook is one of the most accurate prophets I have come across in the many years of acquaintance with prophets and the prophetic. He is a prophet of amazing depth. He speaks with biblical knowledge and firsthand experience of the gift of prophecy. ***Partnering with the Prophetic*** has without a doubt been written under the inspiration of the Holy Spirit and is a textbook of guidance for the generations to come.

There are truths and revelations that provide fresh insight from God's Word. Those operating outside the Church in the business world, media, and daily life will be encouraged to "step into life's arena" and carry the gift of prophecy with them to be shared with a hurting world. I recommend Dr. Bruce Cook's book, ***Partnering with the Prophetic.*** It is a practicum for life and blessing.

Peggy Cole
Peggy Cole Ministries International
www.peggycoleministries.org
Atuskagora, CA

Finally, the one book on the prophetic that I can use both in my graduate level course on 5-Fold Ministry at Regent University, as well as in the equipping ministries in the churches that I oversee. Dr. Bruce Cook has that rare combination of loving God with his whole mind and whole heart so that the reader has the assurance of the combination of integrity of research and the ignition of the Holy Spirit. In a time of traveling light, this is the one book on the prophetic that will give you focus and passion for its full restoration.

Dr. Joseph Umidi
Professor, Overseer, CEO
www.lifeformingcoach.com
Virginia Beach, VA

Partnering with the Prophetic is a fabulous read. It is refreshing in its style and content, full of both personal and practical anecdotes but also powerful in its biblical insight. Bruce Cook takes many divergent threads in the prophetic realm and weaves them into a cohesive tapestry that is profound and yet easy to see and to grasp. This book is strategic and brings needed definition and direction to this vital dimension of the Christian walk. I am grateful to Bruce Cook for his obedience in bringing forth this needed perspective for the Body of Christ at this critical hour.

Dr. Berin Gilfillan
CEO, International School of Ministry (ISOM)
www.isom.org
San Bernardino, CA

Spiritual power comes from the heart and mind of God through the revelation He brings to and through His people. The kingdom of Heaven advances when His will is seen and heard, when His heart is felt, when His word is spoken. Throughout the ages YHWH has used His servants the Prophets to reveal his purposes and His plans for individuals, cities, nations and the whole world.

From generation to generation there have always been those who operated in the gift of prophecy and others who have ministered as prophets, bringing forth a relevant and timely word from God for them. When prophecy became more and more widely accepted during the late 1980's and 1990's a hunger for the word of God was accompanied by a surge of people operating in the prophetic. Sometimes there was a corresponding lack of proper and principled practices taught to those learning this ministry, often resulting in misuse and abuse.

During the last two decades God has been moving in the marketplace in ever-increasing ways. Many leaders are finding out that they have a calling to be Kingdom marketplace ministers, and that they can use their spiritual gifts in the business world, the political realm and in other sectors of the world we live in.

Dr. Bruce Cook has brought to the Body of Christ a book inspired by the Holy Spirit, full of practical, powerful concepts that reveal the inside story of the spiritual dimensions of the prophetic world. Reading and studying these chapters will bring a greater degree of understanding to the Body of Christ and more accountability to those who minister in the prophetic. Studying this book should be considered as a prerequisite to going forth. I highly recommend both the book, *Partnering With the Prophetic* and the author, Dr. Bruce Cook, a modern day prophet full of integrity, wisdom and love.

Duncan Campbell
*Apostolic Missionary and co-founder of Joy Ministry and
Kingdom Marketplace LLC
President of Kingsway Investments and Associated Brokers
www.duncanandwendy.com
Fayetteville, AR*

I am delighted to see works like **Partnering with the Prophetic** come forward, especially from one who has made the personal journey through the prophetic landscape. In a time following a tremendous restoration of the prophetic, clear, mature voices are beginning to emerge from a new generation of prophets. Bruce Cook is representative of this new generation who understands the need and power of partnering with the prophetic. This book is not theory; it is the reality of how the prophetic is to function in our every day lives, businesses and ministries.

Randy DeMain
Founder, Kingdom Revelation Ministries
www.kingdomrevelation.org
Austin, TX

I have known my friend Dr. Bruce Cook for around 10 years and have prophesied over him about as much as he has over me. I have found his ministry true, sincere and accurate. **Partnering With The Prophetic** is not just a book of theory but a practical application of the prophetic gift and the different types of prophecy; this book is about the life of a modern-day businessman AND prophet. In this volume Bruce expounds not just about the prophetic gift but he reveals to us his PROPHETIC LIFE. This is sure to become a companion to other leading books on the subject.

Charles Robinson
W.I.S.E. Ministries International
Workplace. Intercession. Support. Empowerment.
www.coachmybusiness.com
Austin, TX

I just finished reading Bruce Cook's most important new book, ***Partnering with the Prophetic.*** This book truly fills a missing place in all believers' lives. Jesus said that the Holy Spirit would come and show believers things to come. Jesus therein instructed us all to be visionaries, and we all are to be prophetic. Bruce Cook has explained how this happens in our daily lives. He has identified the unifying principles behind being prophetic. With Scriptural facts and incisive analysis, this important work combines biblical thought with today's applied principles. This book reveals a comprehensive fresh way of viewing our prophetic potential.

David Van Koevering
Chief Visionary, Elsewhen
www.elsewhen.com
Cleveland, TN

Bruce is a brilliant man who understands that human brilliance pales in comparison to the divine brilliance that is made available to us through this tool that we call "the prophetic." This book delves into the multiple manifestations and settings of "the prophetic," confirming to us how our God is the God of all life, with a heavenly wisdom available for every sector and situation of life. I wholeheartedly endorse this book by my friend, Dr. Bruce Cook.

Johnny Enlow
Author/Speaker
Rainbow God, The Seven Mountain Prophecy,
The Seven Mountain Mantle
Valencia, CA

Dr. Bruce Cook, out of obedience to The Lord, has written *Partnering With The Prophetic,* a book that will help individual Christians as well as The Church understand and embrace the prophetic voice in our day. He explains how to discern the true from the false, how to listen, judge, receive or reject prophetic words. The Body of Christ needs to be equipped with all of the gifts of God to overcome in this age. A job well done Dr. Cook, you helped me, thank you.

Pastor Steve Hall
Kingdom Fellowship, a Marketplace Ministry
www.kingdomfellowship.org
Jacksonville, FL

Having been involved with the prophetic since the mid 80's when it was less than a frequent experience, I appreciate Dr. Cook's work on the subject for less obvious reasons. The prophetic movement has grown and is becoming more acceptable in regular Kingdom circles. It plays a regular part of spiritual activity in most ministry events. Alongside its growing use, we must have the sensibility to tackle the unanswered yet often-thought questions, such as: "What if the word spoken to me is wrong or tainted? How do I activate the prophetic in me? What are the different types of prophecy both spiritual and carnal that exist and what does the Bible say about it? *Partnering with the Prophetic* is a Handbook for the hungry heart wanting to know the practical way to live in the prophetic. It has great biblical foundations and it addresses the questions everyone is asking in a way that meets every day life. Bruce Cook has the courage to speak the truth in love for all of us to walk into new dimensions with freedom.

Dr. Raymond Larson
Co-Founder & President, 7 Degrees
www.7degrees.org
Austin, TX

It is profoundly refreshing to hear such an important topic explained by a businessman. Bruce's articulation is biblically thorough, balanced, and practically wise. During my pastoral years I was pleasantly surprised to see that all of God's people do hear His voice. They are not fooled by the counterfeit and they resonate greatly with the voice of the Holy Spirit. Learning to use this gift as a tool to build the Kingdom is a huge asset in the marketplace. The simple truth is that we can all "learn" to activate our prophetic ability to hear from the Lord, give words to the light, and bless others. *Partnering with the Prophetic* is a great gift for those ready to take the next step in making the prophetic practical in the marketplace. Thank you, Bruce.

John Garfield
Author, Speaker, Entrepreneur
www.Releasing-Kings.com
Kennewick, WA

I am honored and thankful for the experience of attending and presenting at the annual Kingdom Economic Yearly Summit (K.E.Y.S.) conference. It is from this experience as well as decades of my personal and professional experiences, I am able to identify the strength and power of the prophetic gift Dr. Bruce Cook carries and the great truths which permeate his book, ***Partnering with the Prophetic.*** Therefore, it is with great honor and humility I endorse his work, so clearly birthed by the words of the Holy Spirit to us regarding the principles, practices and protocol of the Prophetic.

Teri Werner
Teri Werner International, Inc.
www.teriwernerinternational.com
Mesquite, TX

In ***Partnering with the Prophetic,*** Bruce Cook presents a compilation of organized thought, biblical references, valuable resources mixed with personal observations, experiences and encounters in an easy to read format that will be useful for the prophetic novice and the prophetic mentor alike. Bruce's sound understanding of the gift of prophecy promotes a wise exercise of the gift and a balanced partnership with the other gifts within the body of believers today.

Dr. Gary L. Sorensen
Co-Founder of Reborne Global Trust
www.propheticeconomics.com
Warriors Park, PA

Dr. Bruce Cook has been mightily used by God to impact the marketplace as well as the church through his spiritual gifts, teaching and godly insights. *Partnering with the Prophetic* is a hands on approach that will bring great fruitfulness to those who glean from its wealth of knowledge. Dr. Cook has poured his expertise into these pages that are filled with revelatory keys. After applying the skills that are available in this book you will be prepared to share a now word with those you meet. God wants to communicate to people through you! *Partnering with the Prophetic* will make you a valuable Kingdom partner that is equipped to advance God's Kingdom through the prophetic now word.

Dr. Barbie L. Breathitt
President, Breath of the Spirit Ministries, Inc.
www.barbiebreathitt.com
North Richland Hills, TX

We have just finished reading your book on *Partnering with the Prophetic*. In thirty years of hands on experience in and study of the Prophetic, this book is the broadest spectrum of balanced and practical revelation we have ever read on the subject. Thank you for your service to the Prophets and the Body of Christ with this work.

Stephen & Julie Bundra
Voice in the Harvest
www.voiceintheharvest.com
San Antonio, TX

Dr. Bruce Cook has packaged the controversial subject of the prophetic and prophecy in a manner that is sure to make former critics of prophecy and prophetic ministry into passionate converts. He has managed to bring academic relevance to the prophetic—a ministry that has been shrouded in mystery, ambiguity and even scandal—along with its proper inheritance as God's gift of love to His dear children during their pilgrimage on earth. On a personal note, Dr. Bruce Cook's blockbuster book ***Partnering with the Prophetic*** leaves me with goose bumps because I am a living testimony to the importance of harnessing prophetic technology to enter into the "God-given destiny!"

It is my personal belief that ***Partnering with the Prophetic*** will become one of the most widely-read books on the subject of the prophetic.

Dr. Francis Myles
CEO, Kingdom Marketplace Coalition LLC
Bestselling author of "The Order of Melchizedek"
www.francismyles.com
Phoenix, AZ

As you read this book you will receive an understanding and activation of the prophetic word of the Lord. I have been greatly blessed by prophetic words I have received through Dr. Bruce Cook. Now you too can discover how to hear and deliver prophetic words with accuracy. I highly recommend this book!

Dr. A.L. "Papa" Gill
President, Gill Ministries
www.gillministries.com
Big Bear Lake, CA

We have just completed Dr. Bruce Cook's new book, *Partnering with the Prophetic,* and we would recommend this book to anyone who desires a deeper understanding of the prophetic and how to partner with the prophetic in both their personal lives and in ministry. Dr. Cook has been able to articulate the simplistic attributes of the prophetic. What we have been doing in practical application, Bruce has been able to bring alive in book form. Well done my friend.

Doug & Rhonda Shutt
Founders
Arm of Hope Ministry
www.armofhope.org
Houston, TX

Dr. Cook has given the Church a powerful and cutting-edge tool that enables us to grasp many prophetic truths. This book is rich with many modern day, life applications. A novice can pick this book up and gain a wide understanding of what a prophet is and how a prophet operates. I have been privileged to utilize this book as a teaching tool in The Samuel School of the Prophets based in Columbus, Georgia. I highly recommend it as a must read for all levels of the prophetic in the spiritual and marketplace arena. This book will inspire and challenge anyone who is a prophet or who wants to partner with the prophetic. It is a book that is needed for this hour.

Sharon O. Billins
Palm Tree International Ministries
Www.sharonbillins.org
Columbus, GA

Prophecy according to Paul in his letter to the Corinthian Church (1 Cor. 12:28) is a Spiritual gift that God has appointed in the Church, that is positioned between the Apostle and the Teacher as it is related to Function.

With the varied divisions of this Spiritual gift, the differences of its ministry and the diversities of its activities, the "Science" of this gift and its gifting must be understood for the effective working of those gifted by God as "inspired preachers and expounders" in the Church.

The importance of synergy within the Spiritual Gifts is of grave importance for the Church to become the manifested Glory of God.

Dr. Cook, in this work, helps the Church to understand the science and synthesis of the Prophetic. The reading and applied use of this book as a reference guide, handbook and/or teaching manual will provide the understanding that will cause the technology needed for the synergistic flow of the spiritual gifts given to the Church to function as a powerful resource to the implementation of the Kingdom of God in the earth.

Dr. Sylvester Paul Brinson III
Governing Apostle, The Apostolic Company
Hope Outreach Ministry Inc.
Chicago, IL
Hope Outreach Ministry International Inc.
Orlando, FL
President, Hope Bible Institute & Seminary
www.homi.me
Hammond, IN

Regardless of what stream or expression of faith you have chosen or experienced, we can all agree that God is still speaking to us today, and He often speaks prophetically through His people. Dr. Bruce Cook has developed an ear to hear what the Spirit is saying and delivers the message in ways that encourage hearts and activate God's plans to the glory of God. In this book, Dr. Cook has written not only about the prophetic methods in which God speaks to His children, but also the various ways that mankind may get in the way of God's unadulterated voice. For anyone that desires to know the many ways that God communicates with His people prophetically, while also being aware of the many pitfalls of humanity in the prophetic realm, I recommend this book to you.

Robert Ricciardelli
Founder & President, Converging Zone Network
Visionary Advancement Strategies
www.convergingzone.com
Kent, WA

Partnering with the Prophetic by Dr. Bruce Cook is an organized and systematic approach to the many dimensions of prophetic ministry. It has substance for veteran prophets and valuable tools for young believers. You will be drawn to read this book again and again as the light of its revelation floods your spirit man.

Dr. Richard Eberiga
Founder and President
Christian Fortress International
www.eberiga.com
San Antonio, TX

As one who ministers prophetically, I'm continually seeking fresh resources to keep the prophetic edge sharp in my own life (as a supplement to the intimate pursuit of the Lord). Dr. Bruce Cook's **Partnering with the Prophetic** is such a book. It's an excellent read for those seeking a synopsis of the "State of the Prophetic" in the Church today. Although my bookshelf contains countless number of books on the prophetic that I've read previously, I still uncovered ample fresh morsels of insight in **Partnering with the Prophetic**—and yes, I do heartily recommend this book!

Brian Francis Hume
President of Dominion Leadership Solutions
& Itinerant Prophetic Revivalist
www.kingdomshifts.com | www.dominionleadershiponline.com
Haymarket, VA

Partnering with the Prophetic is a book for today. The Body of Christ is made richer by clear and purposeful teaching, and in this book Dr. Bruce Cook has succinctly and thoroughly dealt with the many vital areas of prophecy. If prophecy is new to you, this book will break the ground wide open. If you are familiar with the voice of prophecy, this book will resharpen your gift and a prove a great resource for discipling and training others.

Tosh Sturgess
Tosh Sturgess Ministries
www.toshsturgess.org.au
Queensland, AUSTRALIA

Soon there will be another release, a higher level of the prophetic flow in the earth ... a fresh river of the prophetic from the throne of our Lord. It will be deeper, more cutting, more powerful, and filled with more of His wisdom and strategies to influence the Seven Mountains, which are the arts, business, education, family, government, media, religion. This book Jesus anointed Bruce to write, releases further foundation and preparation for the reception and activation of this fresh river to the nations. This new and fresh flow will dredge up, thereby removing the old and bringing up the gold of His spirit, and releasing His plans and purposes through the Body of Christ to the marketplace and to government at all levels.

David Newsome
Cornerstone Christian Fellowship
www.cornerstonechristians.com
Temple, TX

As I read Bruce Cook's new book, **Partnering With The Prophetic**, three very specific aspects truly made an impact on me. This great book is comprehensive, it is inspirational AND it is practical. Having spent over 25 years relating to and ministering with forerunners and pioneers in the apostolic and prophetic, I deeply appreciate a book that can do all three!

Bob D. Long
Founder/Director
Rally Call Ministries
Rally Call Institute
Rally Call Center
www.rallycall.net
Austin, TX

This is excellent material for this and future generations. You have gone deeply into the wells of God and come back with a prize. May this volume be on the shelf and files of every hungry Christian who is hungry for more red meat. May God bless it mightily and abundantly.

Ras Robinson
Author, Speaker, Apostolic Overseer | Fullness in Christ Network
www.fullnessonline.org
Ft. Worth, TX

I so appreciate Bruce's heart and his desire to share and articulate the prophetic spirit which flows so abundantly through him. ***Partnering with the Prophetic*** is a practical explanation of what it means to discern and walk in the prophetic. It applies guidelines and defines different prophetic giftings and provides the reader with a much more diverse understanding of what the prophetic is and what it is not.

Fulton Sheen
CEO, Merging Streams Commonwealth
Director of Isaiah 58:12 | President, Sheen Financial
www.mergingstreamscommonwealth.com
Otsego, MI

Bruce Cook's book, ***Partnering with the Prophetic***, is written from the perspective of a teacher who desires to simplify the mystery of the prophetic for the reader. This book provides a balanced, biblically researched, methical journey through the prophetic that will activate your desire to hear the

Lord's voice on a new level. It is one of those "must reads" for anyone with a desire to hear the Lord more.

Paul L. Cuny
Author, Speaker, President of MarketPlace Leadership International
www.marketplaceleadership.com
Jacksonville, FL

If you are looking to obtain a greater understanding of the sometimes controversial and mostly misunderstood gift of the prophetic—then this book is for you. Dr. Bruce Cook has written a wonderful thesis filled with revelation, insight, and direction. **_Partnering with the Prophetic_** will not only become a cherished book in your library, but an invaluable resource you will continually draw upon.

Dr. John Louis Muratori
Best Selling Author of Money By Design
Founder of MBD Curriculum | Senior Pastor of Calvary Life
www.johnmuratori.com
Dallas, TX | Cheshire, CT

As Bruce is finishing this book, we are watching events unfold in Egypt and the Middle East. As believers we are in a season where the Word of the Lord is not only wanted, it is critical. I believe this book is timely and on target to make us more sensitive to hear God and where He is leading us.

Al Caperna
Chairman, CMC Group and Affirm Global
Director, Called2Business Network
www.affirmglobal.com
www.cmcgp.com
Bowling Green, OH

Partnering with the Prophetic is a book all believers should read, because prophets are not the only ones who need to understand the prophetic. The whole body needs to understand the prophetic and allow the Holy Spirit to move in that way. This will bring clarity and unity to the church. It will give us more power and confidence to do great exploits and change the world around us, as well as release a great understanding to our native people that believe in the prophetic, which they call THE DREAMER. Thank you Bruce, for writing this book.

Dr. Negiel Bigpond
Morning Star Church of All Nations
Co-founder Two Rivers Native American Training Center
www.2-rivers.com
Bixby, OK

Partnering with the Prophetic is an indispensable resource for Pastors and believers who desire to partake in the full counsel of God. Dr. Cook not only lays out the foundational principles by which prophecy is to be expressed and validated, but reveals the full expression of prophetic guidance by God in every influence sphere of society today. This lucid book provides sound biblical teaching, which will enable the Believer to discern and to embrace the gift of prophecy.

Wilhelmien van Nieuwenhuisen
Wilhelmien van Nieuwenhuisen Ministries
www.clarioncallministries.org
Wolfenschiessen NW, SWITZERLAND

reface

P **artnering with the Prophetic** is foundational, not optional, for the Kingdom of God, the body of Christ and the Christian life. Prophecy is a gift from God that according to Scripture is to be desired and sought after and cultivated above other spiritual gifts (1 Cor. 14:1). Scripture clearly says that the testimony or witness of Jesus is the spirit of prophecy (Rev. 19:10). The fact that some Christians have misapplied, mishandled or misunderstood the gift of prophecy is no reason or excuse to throw the baby out with the bathwater. A lack of maturity, pure motives, character, experience, understanding or sound judgment in prophetic ministry does not invalidate or indict Scripture or prophecy — just the one ministering. In fact, there are special blessings and rewards associated with the prophetic, prophets and prophecy (Matt. 10:41; 2 Chron. 20:20).

However, many Christians and ministry leaders fail to heed this biblical instruction and would rather part with prophecy than partner with it. Such critics respond to prophecy, prophets and prophetic expression with a range of ignorance, confusion, contempt, ridicule, mockery, disdain, condescension, doubt, suspicion, skepticism, fear, unbelief, jealousy, control, condemnation, false judgment, prayers amiss, curses, and/or rejection.

Such attitudes and actions grieve and quench the Holy Spirit (Eph. 4:30; 1 Thess. 5:19) and hinder the Kingdom of God from being established, advancing, multiplying and maturing. Scripture is abundantly clear that prophecy and prophets are neither dead nor optional, as some believe and teach, but are rather active in and foundational to the work of the church and the plans and purposes of God (Amos 3:7; Eph. 2:19-20, 1 Cor. 12:27-31). Among the various purposes of prophecy are edification, encouragement and comfort (1 Cor. 14:31). Other purposes include correction, direction, confirmation, activation, initiation, warning, timing and judgment.

Those who teach that prophecy and prophets have ceased and are no longer needed or in existence today, fail to understand adequately the role, purpose and function of the Holy Spirit and the charismatic gifts of the Spirit, as well as the structure and function of the church. 1 Cor. 2:6-16 makes it clear that the Spirit of God conveys the thoughts of God, and the secret wisdom of God, and the deep things of God, so that *"we may understand what God has freely given us"* and that *"we may have the mind of Christ."* Verse 12 states, *"We have not received the spirit of the world but the Spirit who is from God,"* and verse 14 says, ***"The man without the Spirit does not accept the things that come from the Spirit of God, for they are foolishness to him, and he cannot understand them, because they are spiritually discerned"*** (author's emphasis). Rom. 8:14 adds, *"For as many as are led by the Spirit of God, they are the sons of God."* Gal. 4:6 also notes, *"And because you are sons, God* *hath sent forth the Spirit of his Son into your hearts, crying, "Abba, Father."*

This book has been commissioned by the Holy Spirit in the fullness of time to shed additional light on the role and purpose of prophecy and prophetic ministry, and the work of the modern New Testament prophet, and to investigate, illuminate, excavate and correlate some of the patterns, processes, protocols, and portfolios associated with the prophetic. We will also examine the seven levels or dimensions of the prophetic, the twelve main types and classifications of prophecy, and discuss Prophetic Activation, Prophetic Creativity, Prophetic Testing, Prophetic Promises and Prophetic Strategy. In short, this book will explore the technology of prophecy, prophets, and prophetic expression. I have purposely omitted writing chapters on Prophetic Evangelism and Prophetic Dreams because there are already several excellent books published on those subjects, and my purpose in writing this book was to cover new ground that has not yet been explored or written about by others. Suffice it to say that I believe in and practice Prophetic Evangelism and Prophetic Dreams.

There are many others in the body of Christ more senior and experienced than me, and more eminently qualified to write such a book, but the Holy Spirit asked me to do so, and who am I to argue with God or to question His judgment? As Scripture says, *"Obedience is better than sacrifice."* I have learned that God knows me better than I do.

God has a great sense of humor, and ironically, as a fundamentalist, denominational Christian for many years, I had taught against prophecy and the gifts of the Spirit before receiving the baptism of the Spirit and a powerful visitation from Jesus on the same night in January 1995, just weeks after receiving my doctoral degree. During that experience the Lord told me that He was calling me to be a financier of His Kingdom, and He gave me the choice of having a career or a destiny. I gladly chose the destiny and my whole direction shifted. Several months later I received my first prophecy from itinerant prophet Peggy Cole on April 8, 1995, who said that the Lord was calling me to the work of a leader and a prophet, and then almost seven years later, in January 2002, the Holy Spirit released and/or activated the prophetic gift in me when I began attending a nondenominational, charismatic church in Austin, Texas named Glory House, where I attended for 11 years and oversaw the prophetic and marketplace ministries as an elder. The senior minister there, Apostle Mark Henderson, has been ministering prophetically since the 1970's, and helped mentor me in prophecy and apostolic leadership.

On June 22, 2002, about six months after I began seeing visions and receiving interpretations of the visions and hearing God's voice, an itinerant prophet from Kansas named Jess Bielby, who was conducting a weekend series of meetings in Austin, Texas called me out of a crowd and gave me a prophecy that shook me to the core of my being. Included was this word: "The Spirit of the Lord says I've raised you up to walk prophetically, to walk with prophets, to be a part of the prophetic, to walk with pastors, to uphold pastors, to prophesy to churches, to do so many different areas of the prophetic—to exhort, to build up, to tear down, so much more. Know this," says the Lord, "that this has been your calling from the beginning."

After getting over this shock, I immediately bought all the books I could find at the time on prophecy, and devoured them in a few months' time, including the popular set by Bishop Dr. Bill Hamon and several books by Rick Joyner, Steve Thompson, John & Paula Sandford, James Goll, Larry Randolph, Mike Bickle and others.

Preface

After I began to make sense of what was happening, and became comfortable with using the gift, my wife and I then went on a series of weekend road trips to prophetic watering holes and training centers in Toronto, Ont.; Pensacola, Fla.; Charlotte, N.C.; Kansas City, Mo.; Albany, Ore. and Redding, Calif. to learn more about prophecy and observe seasoned prophets in action, and attend their prophetic presbyteries. Through that process, I developed my own distinct prophetic style and voice.

In late 2002 I was ordained in prophetic ministry, and since that time I have been on an amazing adventure with the Holy Spirit. God has opened doors and taken me to places that I never would have dreamed possible, and had me minister to many people in different nations. As a business owner and financial consultant and advisor, however, the majority of my ministry has been in the marketplace, and to business and financial leaders, although I minister in churches, festivals, conferences and summits as well. I was ordained as an apostle in the summer of 2006 and since then have been ministering as a prophetic apostle and apostle-prophet. Beginning in 2008 my wife and I have hosted the annual Kingdom Economic Yearly Summit (K.E.Y.S.) in a number of cities.

So, I am a walking testimony that prophecy is alive and well, and still active in the church today. Since receiving my first prophecy in 1995, which has now been fulfilled, I have personally received numerous other prophecies—perhaps close to a thousand—and I never cease to be amazed at the creativity and accuracy and power and wisdom and love of the Lord expressed through the Holy Spirit flowing through His prophets, of which I am one. I have witnessed many miracles during this time, including the healing of cancer, the restoration of marriages and finances, salvations and rededications, seeing people set free from demonic bondage and oppression, and seeing land and buildings redeemed and occupied, and cities and nations transformed for their intended purpose and destiny.

However, not everyone who receives a prophetic word sees it come to pass, and we will discuss some possible reasons for this, as well as what can be done to accelerate prophecy and to partner with the prophetic.

I invite you now to turn the page and begin this journey of discovery with me. I believe God has some surprises in store for you. I know He did for me as I wrote this, or rather, as I took dictation as His scribe and witness.

Dr. Bruce Cook

Foreword
By Dr. Gordon E. Bradshaw

Can two walk together, except they be agreed? Will a lion roar in the forest, when he hath no prey? Will a young lion cry out of his den, if he hath taken nothing? Can a bird fall in a snare upon the earth, where no gin is for him? Shall one take up a snare from the earth, and have taken nothing at all? Shall a trumpet be blown in the city, and the people not be afraid? Shall there be evil in a city, and the Lord hath not done it? Surely the Lord God will do nothing, but he revealeth his secret unto his servants the prophets. The lion hath roared, who will not fear? The Lord God hath spoken, who can but prophesy?"

Amos 3:3-8 (KJV)

These are potent words...and words that show a powerful and vital pattern for our lives. This pattern is called "cause and effect." Everything we see is an "effect" which resulted from a "cause." There is a powerful agreement between cause and effect and when we learn how to cause things to happen according to God's desires, we'll see the effect of countless victories in our lives and we'll be able to bring the Kingdom of God forward at a greater pace. To do that we must learn one of the spiritual processes that governs cause and effect. It's called "Prophecy." When God speaks, He causes things to happen. When God speaks, *who can but prophesy?*" A prophetic word is a powerful instrument of divine "cause" that sets things in motion.

The prophetic ministry is one of the most powerful instruments of cause and effect known to man. The Bible says that God will do nothing without revealing His secrets to the prophets. When people prophesy, it sets a powerful constructive and corrective dynamic into motion. Prophecy, properly motivated and administered, can change the course of nations. It can deliver multitudes and repair damaged relationships. It can recover lost resources and restore efficiency. Prophecy can reveal powerful strategies that determine the outcome of war. It can discover secrets to the ills of society and develop scientific breakthroughs. In short, the prophetic is essential for the history of mankind.

In order to apply this powerful principle to the lives of men, a question must be asked. *"Can two walk together except they be agreed?"* The Lord seems to think so, and He believes that prophecy is an important link that seals the agreement between Himself and mankind. Often, prophecy is like a "bridge" that fills the void between what God believes and what mankind should believe. Believers become empowered and encouraged to start and finish the work of the Kingdom when the prophetic is applied to their efforts. We become *"workers together with him"* (2 Cor. 6:1). It's a powerful partnership indeed!

Mankind can learn to walk in agreement with God in greater ways when prophetic ministry is properly understood, practiced and utilized. When we walk in agreement with God, our entire lives and everything that we say and do will be changed.

Partnering with the Prophetic is an instrument that will quickly become one of the handbooks of prophetic weaponry in this season. Dr. Bruce Cook, himself an extremely accurate and spiritually sensitive prophetic voice, has put together a manual that "cuts to the chase" in describing prophetic activity in the Earth today. His prophetic ministry is known for activating potential and power in those who receive from him. His experience in multiple arenas of Kingdom life is valuable in understanding the varied dimensions of use that the prophetic ministry touches today. Marketplace leaders, those involved in the governmental and political forums, and those functioning in the ecclesia will be able to move forward in confidence, knowing the structure and order of the prophetic ministry as it exists today.

Dr. Cook has given valuable case studies and biblical examples that will become the backdrop for tremendous prophetic words for the future, as well as to give those who are functioning outside of the normal prophetic paradigm of the church, the opportunity to greatly contribute to the destiny of planet Earth and its people.

I highly recommend this work as a handbook for the Kingdom of God and for all those who believe in ***Partnering with the Prophetic*** today!

Dr. Gordon E. Bradshaw
Governing Apostle – Global Effect Ministries Network
Global Effect Movers & Shakers Network (G.E.M.S. Network)
The "ACTivity Institute" Center for Kingdom Empowerment
www.GEMSnetwork.org
Chicago, IL

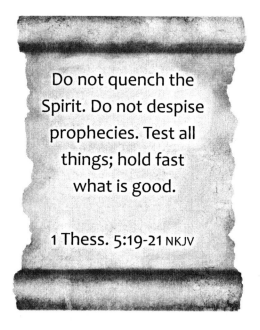

Do not quench the Spirit. Do not despise prophecies. Test all things; hold fast what is good.

1 Thess. 5:19-21 NKJV

Chapter One

Prophetic Style and Voice

I first received a prophetic gift in early 2002. It took me completely by surprise and was not something I had asked God for or ever expected. It came in a couple of different stages over a six-month period. This was my incubation period. First, I received the gift in visual form; then, I received the understanding of what I was seeing, and the translations and interpretations of the different things. Last, I received the gift verbally and words from God began to flow to go with the visions and the interpretations. Those various parts began to be integrated into a seamless whole rather than being disjointed pieces, and I began to be able to work with all three elements at once and to see how they fit together and then have integration of the gift, and that is when the Lord supernaturally launched me into public ministry about four months after that time.

When I first began ministering in the prophetic gift, I read a lot of books on prophecy and most of what was written about it at that time. I also took several road trips to some of the most recognized prophetic centers at the Airport Vineyard in Toronto, Ont. and at MorningStar Ministries in Charlotte, N.C. and then to Bill and Beni

1

Johnson's church (Bethel) in Redding, Calif. and Mike and Diane Bickle's church in Kansas City, Mo. (IHOP), and also to other places where the prophetic was well known and had a history and culture.

Part of my training as a young novice prophet was to observe other prophets. You can learn a lot just by watching established, mature prophets minister. So, I went and watched and studied Graham Cooke, Steve Schultz, Rick Joyner, James Goll, Larry Randolph, Stacey Campbell, Cindy Jacobs, and Patricia King speak, teach and minister. I have also observed Kim Clement and Dr. Mark Chironna minister prophetically through television and Internet.

As I observed these recognized and senior prophets, I went through prophetic presbytery with several of these notable, major, prophetic ministries. I saw how they administered their prophetic presbyteries and teams, and what their rules and protocol were. I learned a lot by that. It was a short season, probably a six-month process. But, through that very short, intense process, I became comfortable with the style of prophetic expression that the Lord has graced me with.

I learned and became confident in the grace that the Lord has given me, and I realized that I, too, was equipped because the Lord just broke me; I mean, He humbled me. The first time I met Graham Cooke, the Lord gave me a vision for him and a few words and said I should go and deliver this to him. I said, "God, he will not know who I am." The Lord had to get me over that fear of man and that was a good way to do it. It was in a safe place and a safe environment and Graham was very gracious and thanked me. The same thing happened the first time I visited IHOP and the Lord gave me a prophetic vision for IHOP and had me deliver it to Kirk Bennett, who graciously received it. A few months later the Holy Spirit had Barbara Wentroble come sit at my table at a ministry event and gave me several visions for her, which I shared with her. The same thing happened with Glenn Miller and Dr. Lance Wallnau and Cindy Jacobs the first time I met them. By then, I was starting to get the idea. This was going to become a way of life so I had better get used to it and get on with the program. My life as I had known it was never going to be the same again.

This whole idea of prophetic style and voice is very important. For Kim Clement, his style of prophecy is through worship. He prophesies through playing the keyboard and through worship and singing. Other people prophesy in different ways, but for every prophet, the Lord has given them their own unique style and voice and way of prophesying. One of the prophets who was an early mentor to me, when he had given someone a word, he would then have them repeat that word back to him and God and say it as a prayer to get it in their spirits and come into agreement with it. That is a powerful technique but I do not do that because that would at least double the amount of time that I spend with each person. So, I am just saying that there are different prophetic styles. You have to find your own prophetic voice and style and what feels natural to you.

> You have to find your own prophetic voice and style.

Really, what God is looking for is unique, trusted voices. He is not looking for parrots. He is not looking for echoes. God has a unique word and He has a unique expression of that word through each prophet. Dr. Bill Hamon and Dr. Sharon Stone prophesy primarily through the *Nabih*, or verbal, dimension of prophecy, although Sharon is also a seer and Dr. Hamon is a church historian. James Goll wrote the book *The Seer*, which differentiates between visual

of prophecy, and describes and defines the visual
ophecy, which includes trances, visions, dreams,
ounters, among other expressions—the *Chazah*
ts.

Prophets (and/or prophet-apostles in a few cases) such as Rick Joyner, Patricia King, Paul Cox, Paul Keith Davis, Shawn Bolz, Kathie Walters, James Goll, Dr. Mahesh Chavda, David Herzog, Sharnael Wolverton, Bill Hart, Randy DeMain, Joshua Mills, Sid Roth, Bobby Conner, Bill Yount, Keith Miller, and others have written a number of books detailing angelic encounters and third heaven experiences and divine visitations. A few examples include *The Final Quest* by Joyner, *Angels That Gather* by Davis, *Keys to Heaven's Economy* by Bolz, and *Living in the Supernatural* by Walters. Joyner, Herzog, King, Jeff Jansen and Ryan Wyatt have regular television and Internet programs with titles such as MorningStar Television, The Glory Zone, Extreme Prophetic and XPmedia, Glory Fire TV, and Abiding Glory, respectively. Sid Roth, a Messianic Jewish believer, hosts radio and television shows called "It's Supernatural" to showcase some of these stories of ordinary believers having extraordinary encounters with angels or with God and seeing divine fruit from it.

Graham Cooke is a teaching prophet with a story-telling style and a keen sense of humor. Dr. James Goll is also a very strong teaching prophet. Both of these men are prolific writers. Kathie Walters has an anointing for angelic encounters and third heaven experiences. Keith Miller is sometimes known as "The Electrician" partly because of his previous occupation before becoming a fulltime evangelist and revivalist, but also because a surge or intense burst of energy or power often flows to accompany his prophecies. Keith and his wife Janet also see frequent healings in their services, as do Shawn Bolz, Tosh Sturgess, and others.

Jack Serra has a prophetic gift of praying for marriages. Dawna DeSilva uses her prophetic gift for inner healing. Wendy Alec has written *The Journal of the Unknown Prophet,* which describes a series of visitations by Jesus with her and conversations about the future. Prophets like Dr. Chuck Pierce and Cindy Jacobs have written books on intercession, warfare, timing, worship, etc. and give prophecies to nations, states or people groups, and Barbara Wentroble has written *Prophetic Intercession.* Cindy is also president of the Apostolic Council of Prophetic Elders. Stacey Campbell leads a similar group in Canada, and has written a book on *Ecstatic Prophecy* that describes the physical state of shaking or vibration she often experiences (ecstasy or ecstatic state) while sharing or delivering a prophetic utterance.

Prophets like Dr. Barbie Breathitt, John Paul Jackson and Doug Addison have a heavy emphasis on dream interpretation and teach prophetic courses and offer training schools. All have written books on dream interpretation. Doug is also a stand-up comedian and has written a book titled *Prophetic Evangelism,* as has Sean Smith. Several prophets publish daily short prophetic words from the Lord to their mailing lists. Among those are Ras and Bev Robinson, Bill and Marsha Burns, and Frances Lloyd. Dr. Negiel Bigpond, Dr. Jay Swallow, Dr. John Benefiel and Jim Chosa understand the importance of prophetic acts and often participate in land repentance and identificational repentance, as do Dr. James Goll and Dr. Tom Schlueter. Bob Long and Will Ford are called to speak into governments as are Alice Patterson and Dr. Clyde Rivers. And, literally millions of Josephs and Daniels, Esthers and Mordecais, Nehemiahs and Cyruses, Lydias and Corneliuses, are in place and on duty in the marketplace and in government, part of a growing nameless, faceless army of God.

A few prophets and/or apostle-prophets offer intercession services to companies and/or ministries, such as Michele Seidler and team with Ancient Paths Inc. and Samuel Company, Charles and Liz Robinson with WISE Ministries, Jeff Ahern and partners with Sozo Services, Jon Grieser with PAGA, Rob Robinson with KBA, Beth Alves with Increase International, Dr. Tommi Femrite with Gatekeepers International and AIN, in London Dr. Richard Fleming, in Australia Dr. Stan Jeffery with Boardroom Prophets, and in Canada, Dennis and Katie Wiedrick, Ralph and Sharon Gerlach, with Divine Exchange.

So, there is a wide variety of expression, gifting and focus among prophets in the body of Christ, and we certainly have not exhausted the subject here. I have been in thousands of ministry meetings over the years, and hundreds of prophetic meetings, including a few all-night meetings where prophets were still prophesying over people when the sun came up the next morning. Some prophets give long prophecies of 30 to 45 minutes per person, and others give much shorter prophecies, sometimes just a sentence or a simple vision. Part of maturing in the gift of prophecy is to find your own prophetic style and voice and *metron* (sphere of rule or authority) and to become comfortable and skilled in knowing how God speaks to and through you to help others. And, make no mistake about it, your gift, mantle, or office has been given primarily to help others rather than yourself.

It is often said that God will take whatever He finds and use it. Nothing could be truer than those words. Whoever you were when you became born again was nothing but an unregenerated version of who you are now. Even though *"all things become new,"* there are still some very concrete character styles and mannerisms in each of us. God doesn't change us so much that we are unrecognizable, but He cleans and enhances us so that we can be useful to the Kingdom.

People often develop prophetic delivery styles that are relative to where you live and what they do for a living. If you live in the southern or northeastern regions of the United States, for example, you'll probably prophesy with a dialect from that region. The same thing is true and applies in China, Australia, New Zealand, Canada, Mexico, India, Africa, the UK and every other place on planet Earth. There is a jargon or terminology or dialect that relates to nearly every country and region on Earth. This adds authenticity to the message and content of prophecy in many cases, though certainly not a strict requirement.

When people prophesy, they reflect their cultures, regions and lifestyles. So, we are not to be men and women without a country, and we are not to be prophets without culture. Rather, we are to bring the culture of heaven and the culture of the Kingdom into the natural culture we live and work in. We are to be in the world but not of the world. That is what Jesus taught in Matthew 13 through a series of parables. We are to be salt and light, and He said a little leaven (yeast) leavens the whole lump (loaf). Part of that process of influencing culture typically involves the prophetic. It is one of the tools, gifts, strategies and weapons God has given His army that sets us apart and guarantees us victory as overcomers, joint heirs and sons and daughters of the Most High in the war with the forces of darkness and evil in which we are engaged.

> We are to bring the culture of heaven and the culture of the Kingdom into the natural culture we live and work in.

2 Cor. 10: 3-4 says, "For though we live in the world, we do not wage war as the world does. The weapons we fight with are not the weapons of the world. On the contrary, they have divine power to demolish strongholds." (NIV) One translation of v. 4 says "the weapons of our warfare are not carnal." Prophecy is one such weapon. And fortunately, we know how the war ends, and we are on the winning side. In the next chapter, we will look at the foundational nature of prophecy.

Chapter Two

Prophecy is Foundational, Not Optional

Many people in the church today as well as in the world are nervous or confused about prophecy and don't seem to understand it. Sometimes they want to ignore it or they want not to honor the prophetic, and not to partner with it. The title of this chapter declares that God has established prophecy in the Bible and in the church and in His Kingdom. He is very clear about that all throughout the Scriptures and Jesus was a prophet. God spoke to all existence to prophesy order and life as we will find out in a later chapter. For the church to fulfill its mission and purpose that Jesus died for, then we have to have prophecy in the church and the church has to learn to accept, embrace and utilize prophecy. Of course, that also will require for the prophets among us to grow up spiritually and to become seasoned and mature and wise about how, why, what, where and when to prophesy, and about how to relate and partner with the rest of the body of Christ.

The proper foundation for prophecy and the prophetic is the Lordship of Jesus. Jesus must be more than Savior in our lives; He must be Lord. That includes his Lordship over our mind, will, and emotions, and our thought life and self-talk. Prophecy is rarely logical, rational or analytical; therefore, it often offends the mind and intellect. We must overcome that and get beyond it and go on to spiritual maturity so that our spirits rule our lives rather than our minds, emotions, or physical appetites.

Scripture is abundantly clear that prophecy and prophets are neither dead nor optional, as some believe and teach, but rather

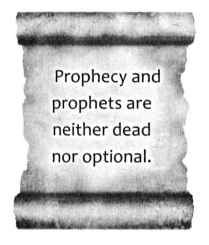

Prophecy and prophets are neither dead nor optional.

are active and foundational to the work of the church and the plans and purposes of God (Amos 3:7; Eph. 2:19-20). Among the various purposes of prophecy are edification, encouragement and comfort (1 Cor. 14:31), to name just a few. Other purposes include correction, direction, confirmation, activation, initiation, warning, timing and judgment.

In an age where prime time television programming includes *The Medium* to showcase the abilities of psychics, and series on zombies, werewolves, and vampire slayers, plus millions more being attracted to New Age theology, it's time to receive, utilize and honor prophecy and prophets in the church as God intended, so that the church stops calling the psychic hotlines and spending billions of dollars a year asking the world for answers that God has already given to His prophets. If we are serious about reforming the culture of the earth, and influencing or ruling the Seven Mountains or spheres of culture, we must first start by reforming the culture of the church, especially in regard to the prophetic.

Those who teach that prophecy and prophets have ceased and are no longer needed or in existence today, fail to understand adequately the role, purpose and function of the Holy Spirit as well as the charismatic gifts of the Spirit. 1 Cor. 2:6-16 makes it clear that the Spirit of God conveys the thoughts of God, and the secret wisdom of God, and the deep things of God, so that *"we may understand what God has freely given us"* and that *"we may have the mind of Christ."* Verse 12 states, *"We have not received the spirit of the world but the Spirit who is from God,"* and verse 14 says, *"The man without the Spirit does not accept the things that come from the Spirit of God, for they are foolishness to him, and he cannot understand them, because they are spiritually discerned."* Rom. 8:14 adds, *"For as many as are led by the Spirit of God, they are the sons of God."* Gal. 4:6 also notes, *"And because you are sons, God hath sent forth the Spirit of his Son into your hearts, crying, Abba, Father."*

Part of being a peculiar people (Titus 2:14, 1 Pet. 2:19) is being a prophetic people. Movies that utilize prophetic symbolism and religious imagery such as the *Star Wars* trilogy and *The Chronicles of Narnia* and *The Matrix* series have tended to do well at the box office, not just because they were well written, well directed and well produced and well marketed, but because they also touched on deep themes of the human soul. Prophecy is more than just foretelling and forthtelling; it is much more complex than that. That is like saying that languages have vowels and consonants. While true, it doesn't tell you much about a particular language.

The prophetic dimension is the audio-visual department of heaven. Most prophecies come through seeing or hearing in various forms. The prophetic gift, like other spiritual gifts, bypasses the mind in order to operate or function, and flows from our spirit. It is spirit to spirit communication. Often people that are trained to be highly analytical such as doctors, lawyers, engineers, accountants, professors and scientists have a harder time accepting, understanding, and/or engaging with prophecy than others.

We must realize that as humans we are tri-partite beings, composed of spirit, soul and body. If any prophetic words are to be expressed verbally, they will have to come through the mind and be processed and delivered through the body and out of the mouth. This works in both positive and negative ways. Believers must practice a consecrated lifestyle, be open to prophetic training and be good students of the Bible in order to establish the foundational discipline that is needed to rightly divide and disseminate prophetic words. Proper training will store information in the mind that will help to establish guidelines for revealing prophetic words in a manner that will reflect credibility and glory toward God. Also, information learned will be a backdrop that we use to form the vocabulary that we prophesy with. Prophetic ministry works a great deal from the memory of previously-stored information and descriptive language.

In his Jumpstart Prophetic Training Course, Dr. G.E. Bradshaw points out that John 14:26 says, *"But the Comforter, which is the Holy Ghost, whom the Father will send in my name, he shall teach you all things, and bring all things to your **remembrance**, whatsoever I have said unto you."* (KJV) The term *remembrance* is taken from the Greek word *hupomimnesko*, meaning — to remind quietly, to suggest to the memory or to put in one's mind (Strong's). This means that the Spirit of the Lord can cause us to recall information previously learned as a vocabulary file from which to draw the language of the prophetic or to reveal words that were learned previously but had been forgotten. In general, people who have limited vocabularies generally prophesy within the limits of their vocabularies. However,

God is not restricted to this and can reveal totally new words or words that we have never known, simply because he is God. In fact, forerunners and reformers often have to invent new terms and coin new language to describe the new thing God is doing.

Best-selling author and pastor Rick Joyner cited a statistic in one of his books several years ago that at least **12 billion dollars a year is spent on psychic hotlines by Christians in the U.S. every year.** That number has probably increased since then. I think this is really an indictment of the modern-day church or at least the Western church of abdicating and shutting out the gift of prophecy in the church, forcing people to look outside the church and seek other methods of hearing from God. In the U.S., we even have TV shows like *The Medium* and *Psych* that are on television as a series.

Hearing from God is so natural. That's why God wants to honor and uncover the gifts because communication is the key. First of all, if you cannot hear from God, if you cannot receive directions from God, and you cannot get the answers to the decisions that you need to make everyday in life from God, His Word and Holy Spirit, then you are going to flounder and struggle. That is why prophecy is so foundational in your faith walk. It is pretty simple; it is like a grace where we are hearing the voice of God and then obeying Him. That can occur in several different expressions. That can be in the audible words of God. It can be verbal, and the hearing dimension, and *Nabih* is the word to describe the prophet and prophecy. But, it can also be *Chazah* or *Chozeh*, a Hebrew word that means seer or vision. *Ra'ah* is a close counterpart. So, people hear from God and they see from God as well and there are different ways that God speaks to us.

Every follower of Jesus can hear His voice and Jesus wants them to hear His voice. The human body mirrors God. God is three-part, consisting of the Father, Son, and the Holy Spirit as the Trinity. Genesis Chapter One says that man is created in the image of God so we are made up of body, soul, and spirit. Even our cells have three primary parts — electron, neutron, and proton —so we are made in God's image at every level.

One analogy that I will use is we are designed like a computer. Computers have hardware and software. We have a physical mainframe which is our body; then we have the spirit. Our spirit is the software so God has designed us with interfaces like we have with computers so that different software programs and hardware devices can communicate with each other. God has made us to have all these ports and GUIs in our spirit, to use modern computer terminology as an analogy.

The whole chapter of 1 Corinthians 2 deals with this, where it says God's spirit speaks to our spirit (and vice versa) and the leading of God is to communicate by the Holy Spirit with the spirit of man. Basically, we have to shut off our mind at times. We have to learn to turn down the noise volume, the clutter volume in our mind and turn up the heart volume and the spirit volume so that the voice of God does not get drowned out as we go about our daily activities.

What does God's voice sound like? John 10:10-14 says that the sheep know the voice of the shepherd and they will not listen to or pay attention to the voice of the stranger. The voice of God is individual to each person. For some people it is like the experience of Elijah in a cave. The voice of God was not in the earthquake; it was not in the wind; it was not in the fire. Then after all these things a still small voice came. I think for the majority of people the majority of the time, the voice of God is a still small voice. It is like an inner prompting. That is why you have to be listening to the Spirit; you have to be attuned and sensitive to His promptings. We have to tune our spirits and our hearts to the frequency of heaven, to the frequency of God's voice.

At first, when you are beginning in prophecy, you may question, 'is that really God' or 'where did that come from?' Sometimes it is just a thought. Sometimes it is an image or impression or an inner knowing. When a thought comes into your mind, you have to judge it. Did that thought come from my flesh, did it come from the devil or was this from God? Heb. 5:14 says that those who are mature, those who have learned and trained themselves by handling the word and gifts of God, can discern between good and evil so they become victorious and overcome the world. As we hear God's voice, as we listen to God's voice, as we step out on faith, and act on what we have heard from our hearts, then God confirms it. You build your faith by hearing God and obeying.

Again, it goes back to the Scripture in John 10. "My sheep hear my voice." There is a certain frequency we just can tell is the voice of God. The voice of God brings peace. There are a couple of different tests that you can use when you hear something and you are discerning and judging. In 1 Corinthians 12, the Bible says He gives us the gift of discerning spirits. Part of using that spiritual gift is to develop an expertise and maturity in being able to discern where these thoughts and voices come from. As you develop the familiarity and as you develop confidence in your hearing ability, you know that it is God because you have peace of mind and an inner witness about it. Then, other trusted people with whom you have shared what you heard from God, will also have a peace and witness about it to establish it. You will receive confirmation about what you heard from other people. There is a joy; there is a quiet confidence and strength that goes with that.

I would say finally that anything that you hear or see from God will never violate the Scriptures and that is very important. Some people who are less mature or just beginning in the prophetic might think, for example, that they heard a nonsensical word to go jump off the Brooklyn Bridge or to set their house on fire. Obviously, that is not from God. We may not always understand what we are hearing, but it cannot violate our conscience or Scripture. Anything from God will not violate your conscience and it is not usually going to hurt other people, although there can be exceptions to that when godly judgment or discipline are involved. These are a few basic tests that you can put around the things that you hear from God.

Located in the Appendix of this book you will find key Scriptures involving prophecy to lay a foundation for our discussion of the prophetic in subsequent chapters. 2 Peter 1:20-21 says, *"Above all, you must understand that no prophecy of Scripture came about by the prophet's own interpretation. For **prophecy never had its origin in the will of man, but men spoke from God as they were carried along by the Holy Spirit"** (NIV, emphasis added).* Other translations say, *"...as they were moved by the Holy Spirit."* The Greek word for **moved** is *"Phero"* — To bear or carry, be driven, led, rushed, upheld (Strong's). So, apparently the Bible was written by writers who were in an ecstatic state at the time.

I encourage you to study the Scriptures located in the Appendix and dig even further to broaden your biblical knowledge and understanding of prophecy.

This concludes our review of why prophecy is foundational rather than optional. In the next chapter we will look at Prophetic Protocols.

Prophetic Protocols

There is a word called *protocol* and this refers to protocols for heads of state or between ambassadors and people that are representing states, governments and kingdoms and things of that nature. There are certain ways to dress, certain places to be seated at dinners, certain types of gifts to give or exchange, and certain ways to address rulers, dignitaries, heads of state, diplomats, and ambassadors. Beyond that, there is basic ministry protocol, so one of the protocols in prophetic ministry is when you make a mistake or if you give some word or vision that was wrong or you missed it, admit it. Usually people make an interpretation mistake or a timing mistake, since those are the most common mistakes in prophecy, but if you blow it and make a mistake, you just need to admit it. Just say, "I missed that; I misinterpreted what I saw or I misunderstood the timing of what I saw; please forgive me."

You just have to remain humble and teachable and correctable and be accountable to other people, either your local pastor or apostle or to other prophets in your ministry, and in that way God will grow you with your gift. Submit yourself to proper authority. I have submitted to the apostolic covering and elders of our ministry where I worship and fellowship. And, that has produced growth and fruit in my life, my family, my business and in my ministry.

I am also accountable to other bodies of leaders in the body of Christ through different groups that I belong to and different relationships that I have. You have to believe in yourself; you have to believe all the things that you hear from God and when God tells you that "you will operate on that level," grab hold of that. I believe as part of prophetic protocol, when you are beginning in prophecy and when you are unseasoned in the prophetic, you might need to ask a few questions occasionally.

Some prophets and prophetic ministers refer to this as prophetic "contamination," where they want to get their own confirmation from God about people and some prophets do not want any information from the people they are ministering to ahead of time or in advance of the ministry. For them, that would be considered contamination, which would be natural knowledge of the person. But, I believe it is sometimes healthy if you are prophesying to a couple, if the Lord does not show you, and it is a man and a woman together. Sometimes it just makes sense that before you start prophesying you'll ask, "Are you two married?' or "Are you a couple?" Also, the Bible says to prophesy according to the measure of faith that you have. So, if you are a novice or beginner or trainee in prophecy and prophetic ministry, your measure of faith may still be

> Don't overstep the limits and boundaries of the grace or gifting that God has given you to steward.

low. I would add to that, prophesy according to the measure of authority and the type of assignment that you have. Don't overstep the limits and boundaries of the grace, gifting or office that God has given you to steward.

It is okay to be vulnerable when you prophesy and do not be afraid to qualify certain things as you minister about what God has shown you. I think it is okay to ask, "Is there anything in particular you would like me to pray for?" Some prophets are not willing to do that. They will just say, "I am only going to speak what the Lord says to me and nothing else," or "Can I tell you what I see for you?" I believe in some situations, if there is a person that is weeping while in your meetings, for example, you might ask if necessary and if God doesn't show you, "Is there a specific issue that God is touching in your life right now or an area of your life that I might be praying about for you?"

I believe these are just matters of judgment and experience and becoming seasoned. Certainly not everyone will need or want to do this when they minister. But, for those who do, it's not a sign of weakness or ineptness or inadequacy. Those type of questions can be safeguards. I think another protocol is prophesying one at a time. Sometimes you may be in meetings with several seasoned, established prophets and if everyone is competing for attention or competing to be the dominant voice in the meeting, it does not work very well.

I believe we should prophesy in order one at a time as Scripture teaches, and let two or three other prophets judge the prophecy. Occasionally it might be necessary to correct a false or carnal prophecy publicly, if it is blatantly harmful or potentially damaging or disruptive, but more often this is better done in private. If sometimes there is a particular theme in a meeting, such as two prophets have prophesied about doors that are going to be opened this year or next month, for example, and if there are three or four words that come forth about open doors, and then someone else has a word or a vision about 'there is turmoil in Korea', then obviously it is not time to prophesy that because that is not what God is doing in that meeting at that time.

What God is talking about in this meeting is He is talking about opening doors because it has been established by the mouth of three or four witnesses from the other prophets. You have to learn when to hold your word and maybe not even give a word that you hear. Sometimes you might have to write the word or vision down on a piece of paper and leave it with the appropriate person or write it in an email and give it to the church or to a person or to a nation in that form. God can still honor and work with that.

You can't always give a word or the vision that you see because it might not fit or flow with what God is doing in a particular situation or meeting. And, sometimes the person in charge of the meeting may not invite prophecy or may not be open to your word being released, or may not trust you or your ministry because they don't know you well enough. Be respectful of authority and submit to the local protocols and house rules and leaders wherever you are ministering unless it violates your conscience, Scripture, or the revelation God has given you. Discuss such things in private rather than in public with the other leaders. Sometimes in ministry you will just have to bite your tongue and pray under your breath in the Spirit when certain things happen that you don't agree with or that quench the anointing or presence of God in a service that you are not in charge of, or are ministering in, or when you hear false doctrine or personal opinion shared from the pulpit or the pew.

Prophetic drama is another protocol issue to discuss. Some people who are attracted to prophetic ministry are addicted to drama (their own), and have a strong need to call attention to themselves. Sometimes they will do so unknowingly and subconsciously, and in other cases they will do so very intentionally and deliberately. Sometimes this drama can be in mannerisms or dress, sometimes it can be in delivery, style, or wording and sometimes it can be in song of the Lord or other form of prophetic expression.

These people have never met a microphone or a stage that they didn't like. Such people are not yet ready to minister publicly and need inner healing or deliverance from issues like performance, abandonment, rejection, insecurity, pride, low self-esteem, grandstanding, exaggeration, or control and manipulation. Insecurity and low self-esteem and perhaps fathering issues, are usually at the root. I worked with one such prophet for five long years and he washed out and gave up on ministry because he wasn't willing to receive correction, make the changes needed, submit to godly counsel and authority, pay the price, and break off unhealthy relationships and habits and soul ties. He had a welfare and entitlement mentality and never got victory over or deliverance from that despite his strong prophetic gift.

Background checks and reference checks are another protocol area. For either good or bad, we live in a litigious society and world, and this occasionally involves prophets and increasingly affects the church. Major ministries led by such well-known media personalities and authors as Rod Parsley and Joyce Meyer have been the targets of recent litigation. Insurance for ministries — once unthinkable or at least optional — is well on its way to becoming mandatory for protection against harassing and frivolous lawsuits as well as more serious claims. Children's ministries, Youth ministries, Singles ministries, and Worship ministries, in particular, have experienced their share of problems over the years with pedofiles and convicted sex offenders being hired by churches, para ministries, and other nonprofits who failed to do adequate background and criminal checks before hiring them. Just look at all the lawsuits the Catholic Church has settled in recent decades.

In terms of the prophetic, you should almost never agree to minister with someone who you do not know well or at all, or don't have a relationship of trust with, or don't have references, referrals, and/or recommendations for. Be especially careful of invitations from so-called ministers in other nations. I learned this lesson the hard way once and by the grace of God I am determined not to repeat it again. Some people just are not who they say they are or claim to be or who they represent themselves as. It doesn't matter how strong or accurate their prophetic gift is or who they claim to know or how much they offer to pay you or how long they claim to have been in ministry or how big the attendance or the offerings are at their meetings. It's far better to be safe than sorry in ministry, as some wolves in sheep's clothing do exist.

> Some people just are not who they say they are or claim to be or who they represent themselves to be.

Don't do it...under any circumstance...for any reason...unless the Holy Spirit directly tells you to do so and confirms that He will bless and protect you and any others involved, and your spiritual covering and spouse (if married) and intercessors are all in agreement. Your reputation and time and relationships are the most valuable assets you possess. Don't risk or jeopardize them for a stranger. There's far too much downside potential. The Bible says to *"know those who labor among you.*" If you don't know them and can't vouch for their character and lifestyle and ministry track record, and don't know who their spiritual covering and accountability is, then run, don't walk, to the nearest exit from such an invitation. There are unfortunately far too many con artists and wolves in sheep's clothing and false prophets in the world, not to mention just spiritually immature or ineffective ministers.

Occasionally I will hedge what I say when I am not 100% sure of something I am getting or receiving in the Spirit for someone. It might not be as strong or as clear as normal, and so might better be categorized as a "prophetic impression" or "prophetic sensing" rather than a prophetic word or vision. In those cases, I either keep my mouth shut and continue praying, or wait for another time or opportunity to minister to that person. Scripture says that *"Mary pondered these things in her heart."* Sometimes we need to ponder what we see and hear from God and reflect on them.

Depending on what I am discerning at the time, and how strong the impression or sensing is (one confirmation from the Spirit is repetition of words or numbers or images), I might say something like, "Excuse me, but I believe I am sensing something for you. Would you mind if I shared it with you?" (Or, "Would you like me to share it with you?") So, don't be afraid or ashamed to clarify occasionally with someone that you're not sure if what you are sensing or feeling or discerning for them is a prophecy or not. It's better to be safe than sorry. Scripture says, *"If any man speak, let him speak as the oracles of God"* (1 Peter 4:11). The Greek word for **oracles** is *Logion*, meaning: Fluent utterance of God (Strong's). The word fluent implies "full" or "rich" or "masterful" or "complete."

I like what The Message translation says in 1 Samuel 3:19-21, *"Samuel grew up. GOD was with him, and **Samuel's prophetic***

23

record was flawless. *Everyone in Israel, from Dan in the north to Beersheba in the south, recognized that* **Samuel was the real thing—a true prophet of God.** GOD *continued to show up at Shiloh, revealed through his word to Samuel at Shiloh"* (author's emphasis). This provides a good model and should be our goal and aim in prophetic ministry. The NIV translation says that *"The Lord..."* let *none of his words fall to the ground."* The Amplified and King James versions of this passage say that everyone in Israel knew that Samuel was **established** as a prophet. How did they know that? There was accuracy, anointing, power and authority in his words and visions, and they came to pass. People that are risk averse or risk intolerant or that can't handle or deal with uncertainty will probably struggle with the prophetic and not do well with it. Faith is required to be pleasing to God and faith involves trust, risk and action. Obedience is better than sacrifice, comfort or safety.

Another protocol is to record the prophecies you give whenever possible (that is different than whenever you feel like it). I think this is an excellent way to help people grow and for us to be accountable and be good stewards because in this way people can remember them and study their prophecies and share them and pray over them. People can transcribe them and pray over their prophecies and they can show them to other people they trust or look up to like their pastor, apostle, or a spiritual covering. It also might help you keep from being sued or attacked if someone claims that they are supposed to divorce their wife or husband because of the prophecy they received from you or your ministry, when you or your team actually did not say anything vaguely or remotely like that in the prophecy, so it is good to take time to record prophecies with digital recorders and then email the words; it is easy to do that with the affordable and portable digital technology readily available today.

Another protocol is that it is not always necessary to preface your words or visions for people with "The Spirit of the Lord says to you..." Sometimes if the person has no religious frame of reference or has been deeply wounded or traumatized in the past by an authority figure, you might just say, "I believe I am hearing (or seeing or sensing) something for you. Would you like me to (or mind if I) share it?" That is a much more natural and less threatening and intimidating and religious approach for people not familiar with or accustomed to prophecy.

Also, once you release a word from God, you are no longer responsible for it. You have done your job and completed your assignment as far as that word or vision goes. The rest is up to the Holy Spirit and the person or group or entity who received the word. Don't enable them and become their quasi Holy Spirit. Don't become emotionally entangled unless you are giving them God's love, comfort or mercy as part of the prophetic ministry.

It is possible to become addicted to prophecy rather than encouraged, empowered and/or enlightened by it. Some people can become prophetic "junkies" or "groupies," in the same way that there can be pastoral or apostolic junkies or groupies, who follow a particular prophet or group of prophets from meeting to meeting and/or city to city. Such people are immature and are worshipping the gift or personality rather than the giver, and they have become overly dependent on prophecy as a crutch rather than a springboard for their life. Prophetic ministers must resist and discourage any such unhealthy

Prophecy is a gift, a tool, and a weapon.

relationships, no matter how well-intended. Otherwise, it can lead to or become idolatry.

Prophecy is a gift, a tool, and a weapon, but it is not a drug, and it is not a substitute for faith; however, it is designed and intended to enhance and strengthen faith in the believer. Prophecy is also intended to complement a knowledge of Scripture and personal spiritual maturity and character development, not replace them. Michael Sullivant summarized succinctly some of these points as follows in a book titled *Prophetic Etiquette* (1996, pp. 17-18, Metro Christian Fellowship: Kansas City, MO):

> *"For many, the prophetic seems to be a short-cut to guidance in contrast with the longer route of praying, searching the Scriptures, receiving wise counsel, suffering, character building, learning from experience and so forth. The truth is, as most people experienced in the prophetic could testify, this gift rarely works to guide the gifted persons themselves. It is usually given by the Spirit to minister confirmation to others. This is often very frustrating to prophetically gifted people. God just isn't in as much of a hurry or panic to guide us as we usually are to get guided! He is 'into' the journey as much as He is the destination. He is both a glorious intruder and a patient farmer.*
>
> *Sometimes the Lord does graciously intervene with a prophetic word that gives us clear direction. He seems to do this more for some than for others. But be aware that as you start down the pathway, you will wish He would say more than He has! Prophecy is no substitute for walking by faith. We are called to walk by faith, not*

by sight. Some people lust after prophecy thinking that it will eliminate all uncertainty in their lives. Don't buy it. Seeing something prophetically by the Spirit will often signal the coming of more uncertainties and testings into your life than ever and you will need more raw faith to hold the course than you ever expected. Seek to be guided by the more tried and true methods pioneered by the saints throughout the ages and rejoice when the Spirit serendipitously intervenes with a clear word of prophecy to encourage you along the way.

This concludes our overview on Prophetic Protocols and we now turn our attention to Prophetic Processes in the next chapter.

For prophecy never had its origin in the human will, but prophets, though human, spoke from God as they were carried along by the Holy Spirit.

2 Peter 1:21 NKJV

$\mathscr{P}$rophetic Processes

N ext we come to the area of Prophetic Processes, which gets into what I mentioned earlier about the two most common mistakes in prophecy being mistakes of interpretation and timing. I would estimate that probably 90% of all mistakes in the prophetic are made in one of those two areas. Many people in the Western World and in the United States are looking for "McProphecy" rather than real prophecy; they are looking for prophecy on demand— instant prophecy that comes to pass like popcorn popping—or microwave prophecy that comes to pass in one to ten minutes.

That is unrealistic and demonstrates an unhealthy expectation about God. It also displays ignorance of how prophecy works and really about the basics and purpose of prophecy. An instant prophecy example is when Jesus told Peter that *"you will deny me three times before the cock crows twice"* (Mark 14:30, 72); that happened (was fulfilled) within 24 hours. I would just say that is a rarity; that is the exception and not the rule or norm, although it can happen. Most prophecies have a "shelf life" and a fulfillment timeline or timetable associated with them. God is not a prophetic slot machine. So, part of the role of a prophet is to disabuse people of these unhealthy and unrealistic notions — really fantasies — about what prophecy is and how it works.

We have to understand that since God is outside of time, He is an *atemporal* God. He is not locked in the attic or in a box. He's more into *kairos* than *chronos* time. In the Scripture it says that a thousand years is just a day to God. Obviously a person's lifespan is considerably less than a thousand years in most cases and so our whole lifespan is less than a day to God. A person's entire life then might be only an hour or two in God's sight.

He just sees things differently than we do. So, we have to understand that in our prophecies, the prophecies are not always fulfilled in a person's lifetime or generation. The fullness of the covenantal prophecy is not what Abraham and David received; these were not all fulfilled in their lifetimes, but because some of these prophecies were generational, they could only be fulfilled in subsequent generations to receive the fullness that God had intended and promised.

In my own life, it took 13 years for the first prophecy I received to be fulfilled. Part of the prophecy was about becoming a leader and leading a movement. That really only happened when God gave me a vision and commission for convening K.E.Y.S. in early 2008, even though I received the prophecy about this in 1995. So, you should expect that there will be a process with your prophecy.

Joseph had to wait 13 years for his dreams to be fulfilled, and some like Abraham and David, whose prophecies involved future generations, did not live to see them fulfilled. Some prophecies have taken as little as three days, three weeks or three months to come to pass. Those are the exception rather than the norm. Many other personal prophecies are yet to be fulfilled in my life. The majority of them require a process of years or decades to be fully manifested.

Scripture says that Jesus lived and died and was resurrected in the fullness of time. Your prophecies, and their fulfillment, will also come in the fullness of time. We cannot make our prophecies come to pass, but we can partner with them in faith, and we can accelerate or delay or hinder or prevent them from happening by our lack of

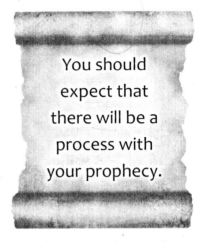

You should expect that there will be a process with your prophecy.

faith. We should adopt an attitude of expectation, humility, and patience regarding prophecy, but sometimes preparation is also needed. For example, a person receiving a prophecy about an entrepreneurial calling may choose to get a business degree from college or take a few courses or apply for an internship. This is not a requirement for the word to be fulfilled, but the person is giving God something to work with.

Presumption is also a common response to prophecy. A person who receives a prophecy about a job change or a future marriage or a new house may accept the next proposal that comes along or may take the next job offer or go house shopping. There is a fine line sometimes between presumption and obedience, and we need wisdom and discernment to know the difference. Fear will paralyze you, and lie to you, and hinder and limit your usefulness. Among the first steps in becoming useful in prophetic ministry is to deal with or kill fear in ourselves—fear of man, fear of failure, fear of rejection, fear of not making sense, fear of sounding stupid or appearing foolish, fear of offending someone, fear of being wrong or making a mistake, fear of embarrassment, fear of not being perfect, fear of not hearing God, fear of not understanding what you see or hear from God, fear of not being qualified, fear of not being worthy or skilled enough, etc.

There are also people who try to make their prophecy come to pass before its time. I would say that these people use presumption with prophecy. They try to run ahead of their prophecies and have their prophecies fulfilled now. When they see something that looks like it might be their prophecy being fulfilled, they jump on it with both feet and really work it and try to make it happen, even when it may be something that God will not make happen either now or ever. So, the better approach is to be engaged with your prophecies and certainly be engaged in opportunities that look like they might be what God is doing. But, wait for a confirmation. Everything that God does is established at the mouth of two or three witnesses (Deut. 19:15, Matt. 18:16). Scripture is very clear on that and He will establish when it is time for your prophecy to come to pass.

One of the primary purposes of prophecy is **confirmation**. Not all prophecy is confirming but the majority will likely be. You should usually receive an "inner witness" as a prophetic word is being spoken if it is accurate or applies to you. In contrast, if you receive a prophecy that does not seem to fit or apply to you or that is extremely judgmental or harsh in tone, you will likely receive a "check" in your spirit that something is wrong with either the word being given or the person giving the word. God's word produces peace and joy and is life-giving. If you become agitated or lose your peace and joy while receiving a prophecy, it is probably a good indication that either the word is not from God, or that the word contains a mixture of spirit and flesh, or that the person giving the word is spiritually immature or inexperienced with prophecy, or that you are having an emotional or demonic reaction and something is being stirred up inside of you.

A few verses that touch on or address prophetic **confirmation** include 2 Peter 1:19, Job 28:27, Daniel 9:12, Isaiah 44:26. 2 Peter 1:19 states, *"We have also a more sure word of prophecy..."* The NIV version says, *"And we have the word of the prophets made more certain..."* The Greek word for **More** is *"Meizon"* from the word *"Megas,"* meaning: Larger or greater. The Greek word for **Sure** is *"Bebaios"* from the word *"Basis,"* meaning: Stable, firm, steadfast, forceful (Strong's). In other words, as New Testament disciples and followers of Christ, we have access to confirmed words that have stronger and greater influence and stability because they are foundationally built by God Himself and have the force necessary to complete the plan and purposes of God.

In Daniel 9:12 and Isaiah 44:26, the Hebrew word for confirmed or confirmeth is *"Quwm,"* meaning: "To make clear, continue, decree, make good, ordain, perform, raise up, remain, establish, succeed" (Strong's). The words of the Lord are, in themselves, a decree that affects the DNA and atomic structure of everything that is created. He causes the motives and intents of His will and purpose to be made clear after what He says demonstrates itself before the eyes of men. What He says will produce His desires. (See **Isaiah 46:10:** *"Declaring the end from the beginning, and from ancient times the things that are not done, saying, My counsel shall stand, and I will do all my pleasures."*) Isaiah 44:26 says *"...That confirmeth the word of his servant, and performeth the counsel of his messengers..."* The Hebrew word for **Performeth** is *"Shalam,"* meaning: To be safe in mind, body or estate; to cause to be complete; to reciprocate; to prosper, make recompense and restitution (Strong's).

In the NIV version, Isaiah 44:24-26 reads, *"This is what the Lord says—Your Redeemer, who formed you in the womb; I am the Lord, who has made all things, who alone stretched out the heavens, who spread out the earth by myself, who foils the signs of false prophets and makes fools of diviners, who overthrows the learning of the wise and turns it into nonsense, who carries out the words of his servants and fulfills the predictions of his messengers..."* The fact that the Lord says He **performs, carries out**, and **fulfills** the words of His true prophets is a powerful statement and testimony about the relationship between God, His spoken Word, and His true prophets. It also indicates the seriousness and spiritual gravity involved in speaking on behalf of the Lord.

Apparently confirmation is important to God and He also finds it necessary and prudent to confirm things. Job 28:27 says, *"He looked at wisdom and appraised it; **He confirmed it and tested it.**"* (NIV, *author's emphasis*) So, even when Wisdom was brought forth as the first of God's works, before His deeds of old (Prov. 8:22-31), God did not stop there. He appraised it, confirmed it, and tested it. He confirmed that Wisdom worked and functioned the way it was designed to work and did what it was created and designed to do. Isaiah 55:10-11 says, *"As the rain and the snow come down from heaven, and do not return to it without watering the earth and making it bud and flourish, so that it yields seed for the sower and bread for the eater, so is my word that goes out from my mouth: **it will not return to me empty, but will accomplish what I desire and achieve the purpose** for which I sent it."* God's word will not return void; it is active and powerful and will

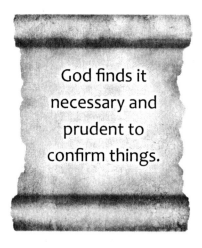

God finds it necessary and prudent to confirm things.

be fulfilled. Hebrews 4:12 says, "*For the word of God is living and active. Sharper than any double-edged sword, it penetrates even to dividing soul and spirit, joints and marrow; it judges the thoughts and attitudes of the heart.*"

Similarly, God confirms His words and the words of His prophets, which are one and the same for those who are true prophets like Samuel ("*none of his words fell to the ground*") and John the Baptist ("*among men no greater prophet has arisen*"). Perhaps the most dramatic confirmation of a prophet in Scripture is Moses as found here in Numbers 12:6-8:

> *"When there is a prophet among you, I, the LORD, reveal myself to them in visions, I speak to them in dreams. But this is not true of my servant Moses; he is faithful in all my house. With him I speak face to face, clearly and not in riddles; he sees the form of the LORD. Why then were you not afraid to speak against my servant Moses?"*

A similar but even more powerful term and concept than confirmation is **establishment**. In the case of Job 22:28, where it says to decree a thing and He will **establish** it, the word used there is **quwm**, meaning to abide, accomplish, be clear, continue, confirm, decree, endure, make good, help, hold, raise, remain, lift up, strengthen (Strong's). And in 2 Chron. 20:20 and 1 Sam. 3:20, the word used for **establish** is **'aman**, meaning to build up or support, to foster as a parent or nurse, to trust or believe, to be permanent or quiet, true or certain, to go to the right hand (Strong's). 2 Chron. 20:20 says in part that if you believe His prophets, you shall be established. 1 Sam 3:20 says that Samuel was established as a prophet of the Lord. God establishes His Words to give them a greater weight of authority for our benefit.

This concludes our study of Prophetic Processes. In the next chapter we will examine Prophetic Strategy.

"God is not a man, that
He should lie,
Nor a son of man, that
He should repent.
Has He said, and will He
not do?
Or has He spoken, and
will He not make it
good?"
Numbers 23:19 NKJV

Chapter Five

Prophetic Strategy

S trategy is an informed and intelligent plan of action designed to produce a desired outcome. God is the ultimate strategist and is still the top strategy consultant in the universe today, although His methods are sometimes unorthodox and may offend our minds, and His flat fee rate is quite high (total obedience even to the point of death). God's strategy for Abraham becoming the father of nations was for Abraham to sacrifice his son Isaac, the child of promise, as a test of obedience (Gen. 22:9-19). Abraham passed the test and the rest is history.

Prov. 8:14-15 outlines the critical role that wisdom plays in the life of the righteous. Wisdom is even listed as the first of God's works (Prov. 8:22-23). Isaiah 55:8-9 says, "'For my thoughts are not your thoughts, neither are your ways my ways,' declares the Lord. 'As the heavens are higher than the earth, so are my ways higher than your ways and my thoughts than your thoughts.'" So, we need to inquire of God to learn His thoughts. Jeremiah 29:11 adds, "'For I know the *plans I have for you,' declares the Lord, 'plans to prosper you and not to harm you, plans to give you hope and a future.'"*

David received direction, instruction, and strategy from the Lord for His military campaigns and battles. On one occasion he was told to pursue and he would recover all (1 Sam. 30:8). On another occasion, he was told not to attack until he heard the sound of marching in the balsam and mulberry trees (2 Sam. 5:24; 1 Chron. 14:15). Another time the armies of Judah, Israel and Edom ran out of water after a seven days march enroute to attack Moab. They were saved and victorious only after Elisha the Prophet intervened and prayed and then shared God's counsel and told them what to do and they obeyed (2 Kings 3:1-27) and it rained the next day.

Another of God's generals, Gideon, was also given strategy as an instruction. He was told to dismiss and send home those troops who were afraid and then to reduce his army to those who lapped water with their hands or tongue like an animal so that God would get the glory for the victory, and then Gideon had those 300 remaining troops surround the camp of the enemy on three sides and use torches, pitchers and horns (shofars) at night to frighten the enemy so badly that 120,000 enemy troops mistakenly slaughtered themselves (Judges 7 and 8), and the rest were defeated or destroyed the next day. Jesus told the disciples to go to Jerusalem and tarry and wait for the Holy Spirit baptism before they continued their ministry after his death and resurrection (Acts 1:4-5, 8). God has strategies for your business enterprises or ministries. Just ask him.

Joshua was told to march the Israelite army around Jericho for seven days and to blow the ram's horns, and then to have the people shout on the last day. When they did that the walls of the city fell down and the city was destroyed and burned with fire (Joshua 6:1-25). Elisha told Naaman to go dip seven times in the Jordan River to be healed of leprosy. Although Naaman was offended by the request and became angry, after receiving counsel from his entourage, he obeyed and was instantly healed (2 Kings 5:1-19).

Elisha overheard the plans of the enemy of Israel, the King of Aram, and reported them so that Israel was repeatedly victorious and Aram was repeatedly thwarted. Finally, the King of Aram had had enough. The king sent his massive army to capture or kill Elisha, but God sent an angelic host to surround the army of Aram and protect Elisha. The enemy's army was blinded by the Lord and Elisha was left unharmed (2 Kings 6:8-23). Similarly, God continues to provide spiritual intelligence to His prophets today.

Several years ago a friend of mine in the San Diego area asked me to pray for a missing 16-year-old high school girl named Colleen from his city, whose car had been found parked in a lot next to a jogging track. I prayed several times for her over the course of several days, but all I kept hearing was the same thing: "Colleen is by the creek." I reported this to my friend, and asked him to notify the police, and a few days later he told me that Colleen's body had been found by police at a nearby creek. This word took faith on my part to release, because San Diego has a desert climate, averaging only 10 inches of rain per year, and I did not know if there were any creeks there.

It is a shame and an indictment on the church and on Western culture that police departments and intelligence agencies choose to consult with psychics and mediums, rather than the prophets of God. Fortunately, there are some exceptions. One of my friends who is an apostle-prophet had a dream several years ago about a burning bush. He discerned by the Spirit that this was a warning dream for the U.S. president at the time to thwart an assassination attempt on foreign soil, and this information was relayed through intelligence back channels. The next day my friend received a call from an intelligence agency officer and was thoroughly questioned. As a result, the president's itinerary was changed that week and disaster was averted, as a suicide bombing in a Muslim nation occurred within days in the city where the President had been scheduled to visit.

Another example of prophetic technology in action occurred in 2003. A prophet in the Western U.S. had a vision and saw a bomb being placed under a strategic Interstate overpass in a Western state where several roads converge. He saw the details so clearly that he was able to identify and locate the spot in the natural. Then he called a friend who notified security and intelligence agencies, and when they searched the area, a bomb was found and deactivated. This type of prophetic warning and accuracy happens more often than most of us need or would like to know, and obviously the vast majority of such incidents cannot be disclosed publicly for security and public safety reasons.

Prophetic Strategy is very important. It is a very powerful dimension in the prophetic and one of the more interesting examples is found in the life of David. He received direct strategy on military plans and tactics for approaching battles as a general and as a king. On one occasion David was told not to attack until he heard the sound of marching in the balsam and mulberry trees. That is a very specific word about timing. I prefer to call it a prophetic strategy, but it's an "aha" moment that is ac-

Prophetic strategy is very important.

tually a specific directional word of how to maybe implement or approach whatever it is that you are doing. It could be a strategy in business, it could be a strategy in the ministry, or it could be a strategy in the military in terms of the example I just gave of King David.

I heard of an example of a U.S. soldier who was driving an armored personnel carrier in Iraq during the current war. He was leading a column of other vehicles and was driving along a road in a region known for terrorist activity. Suddenly, he heard a voice speak to him and say, "Veer over to the right shoulder now." He kept driving and the voice spoke louder. "Get all the way over to the right side of the road now." After hearing this a third time, the soldier steered his vehicle to the right shoulder of the road they were on, and the other vehicles in the column followed suit. The officer in charge radioed the driver and asked what he was doing. After the driver reported what he had heard, the commanding officer ordered a search of the area and a large IED (Improvised Explosive Device) was found planted in the road just ahead. Had the driver not obeyed, there would have been severe consequences and casualties. The driver was commended for his actions by the commanding officer.

Another example would be the life of Gideon. Gideon assembled a small army to resist the Midianites. The initial number of that group of men was apparently 32,000 and then God gave him two strategies of how to reduce the size of the army so that God would get the credit and glory for the victory He had planned for Gideon. The first strategy is that He asked Gideon to ask the army if anyone was afraid, and to send those home and release them from service. Twenty-two thousand left and after that, there were 10,000 troops left. Then God said to take those 10,000 troops to the water and I want you to watch and see how people drink the water and separate them into two groups. There were those who got down on their knees and lapped the water like an animal and those who used their hands to cup the water, and from that 9,700 were released and that left only 300 men.

Then God said take that group; that size I can work with. These 300 men who lapped would go and defeat a vast enemy army. The exact number of the opposing force is not given in Scripture, but this description is provided: *"The Midianites, the Amalekites and all the other eastern peoples had settled in the valley, thick as locusts. Their camels could no more be counted than the sand on the seashore."* Sounds like the odds were pretty uneven. During that night the Lord spoke to Gideon and said, *"Get up, go down against the camp, because I am going to give it into your hands. If you are afraid to attack, go down to the camp with your servant Purah and listen to what they are saying. Afterward, you will be encouraged to attack the camp"* (Judges 7:9-11).

So, Gideon and his servant went to the outposts of the enemy camp and overheard two soldiers talking. One shared a dream he had just had and the other gave its interpretation, which was: *"This can be nothing other than the sword of Gideon son of Joash, the Israelite. God has given the Midianites and the whole camp into his hands"* (v. 14). After Gideon worshiped God, he returned to his camp and dispatched the 300 soldiers into three groups of 100 each. They positioned themselves on the three sides of the opposing troops. Every man was with a torch, a pitcher, a trumpet and a sword. Upon Gideon's command, they lit the torches, broke the pitchers and blew the horns.

When they did that, it startled and scared the enemy. They surprised and disturbed the Midianite army at the beginning of the fourth watch and the enemy in fear and confusion started to kill themselves because they were so frightened and panicked. Some others fled and Gideon pursued and summoned reinforcements to go before the fleeing enemy and cut off their retreat. So, God gave a great military victory to Gideon and Israel through a few key prophetic strategies and a dream and its interpretation.

In the Old Testament, Joshua was told to march around Jericho. No general would just choose to march on Jericho for seven days. That would be foolishness in terms of military strategy but because God said that they had to do it. They marched around once a day for six days in silence and then seven times on the seventh day and the people let loose a shout and a roar and you know what happened next; the walls fell down and God gave the city into their hands . God uses the foolish to confound the wise.

So, God is a strategist and God has a strategy or strategies for your business and/or ministry. God has a strategy for your life, for your finances, for your marriage, for everything that you are doing and you simply have to ask Him, listen and receive, and then obey. So, strategies are an important part of partnering with the prophetic. In the next chapter, we will look at Prophetic Intercession.

So shall My word be that goes forth from My mouth; It shall not return to Me void, But it shall accomplish what I please, And it shall prosper in the thing for which I sent it.

Isaiah 55:11 NKJV

Chapter Six

Prophetic Intercession

It has been said by several ministers I know that all prophets are intercessors but not all intercessors are prophets, and I believe there is truth in this statement. Certainly one of the hallmarks of a mature prophet is an intimate relationship with God the Father, God the Son, and God the Holy Spirit. Such intimacy includes frequent times of prayer and communion, and for many, fasting and worship.

God began to teach me about intercession around nine or ten years ago through a series of events. I had been operating a business for six years after 25 years of working for other companies and was just preparing to launch an investment fund with a few like-minded Christian businessmen. The Lord spoke to me that I would need an intercession team. "What's that?" I naively asked God. So, I began asking a few people in my network if they knew any intercession leaders and anything about intercession.

Shortly thereafter, I identified someone locally who had led intercession before and arranged to meet them with a third party as a witness just to be safe, since it was a female. We visited for an hour or so to get acquainted and compare visions and I asked her to pray about forming an intercession team to pray for my family and businesses, and left. When she accepted a few days later, my education on intercession began. We started with four or five people meeting several times a month in the evening to pray corporately, then the group grew in number over the next year and just as quickly reduced when the intercession leader felt called to focus on her own ministry and moved to another city.

The next phase began when I decided to build another intercession team and lead it myself. That lasted around one year and got up to around 100 intercessors using the prayer shield model. I had read several books on intercession by that time and had attended an intercession workshop lead by Tommi Femrite and Billie Boatwright which focused on the 12 types or styles of intercession. The prayer shield model, while effective, took a lot of work and I didn't always have time to focus on it with my other responsibilities. Then I met someone (another Kingdom businessman) from another country and we connected in the spirit and he introduced me to someone he knew in business in the U.S. who had a calling to pray and lead strategic intercession assignments.

From the first phone call I had with this individual in late 2007, there was an instant connection in the spirit and a supernatural ability to communicate and on multiple occasions since then, to have corporate (collective or joint) spiritual experiences on earth or third heaven experiences together in different rooms in heaven where we were both seeing and experiencing the same thing at the same time though separated physically by thousands of miles.

We sensed we were supposed to do something together in the Kingdom and he offered to pray for me. Then a few months later, in early 2008, the Lord commissioned me to convene the Kingdom Economic Yearly Summit (KEYS). My new friend, a financial advisor and wealth manager, agreed to take over intercession for KEYS and provide leadership and oversight to the core intercession group on a volunteer basis. Since that time there have been many prayers and many strategies and many prophecies that have come forth from this group, and my understanding of intercession has increased dramatically. In fact, I have helped lead or co-lead intercession for several boards that I have served on in the past few years.

To give a quick example of the power of intercession, one Thursday night I was attending our weekly church service and I was minding my own business when the Holy Spirit spoke to me clearly and distinctly and said, "Begin praying right now for the soul of Yassar Arafat." I thought that was a somewhat strange request from God, but I have learned to be obedient and not question His ways, which often seem unusual and at times outrageous to my mind but are acceptable and usually delightful to my spirit. There was an urgency about this directive, and so immediately I shifted into gear and began interceding earnestly for the soul of this now deceased, internationally-known, feared and hated terrorist, who at the time was the leader of the Palestine Liberation Army (PLO) and was undergoing medical treatment for a serious illness. I also shared this new assignment with our small church and a corporate prayer

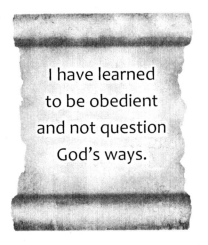

I have learned to be obedient and not question God's ways.

of agreement was quickly spoken. I continued praying for several hours and then left for home. Two days later I heard on the news that Yassar Arafat had died.

I assumed that was the end of the story and the assignment. Several years later I was at a meeting in a different city and state and the speaker was R.C. Kendall. I had never met R.C. and was stunned when he mentioned during his remarks that he had been given the privilege to accompany the Archbishop of Canterbury to visit Yassar Arafat only a few days before his death, and even though Arafat was never alone and without guards and others around him, they had been able to share the Gospel with Arafat. So, now years later, this intercession assignment suddenly took on new meaning and significance.

On another occasion several years ago, I was invited to the United Nations Prayer Summit by another ministry leader. Due to pressing business responsibilities and obligations, I was not sure whether to accept this invitation or not. In prayer one day as I was telling God why I could not make this trip, He spoke to me and said, "I not only want you to go, but I want you to take your pastor as your guest and pay for all of his expenses." With that instruction, I confirmed our attendance with the host, invited my pastor, bought plane tickets and made hotel reservations, and prepared for the trip.

On the flight from Texas to New York as I was in prayer, the Holy Spirit suddenly gave me a vision of a man with a thin moustache and short-cropped hair on the sides and back of his head and bald on top who had an authoritative look about him and was carrying two 12-packs of clear liquid in plastic bottles, one in each hand. The two 12-packs had plastic carrying handles on top so it was easier for the man to carry this weight. The number 12 immediately caught my attention and I realized this man had a governmental mandate and assignment, and the two 12's seemed to mean double portion or global measure. One of the more interesting details in this vision was that each of the 24 bottles had writing on its respective label in a different language. The Holy Spirit told me that each bottle represented a different nation, and the interpretation was that this man was carrying nations. Of course, water can represent life or the Spirit and so this man was carrying the Spirit into different nations. The vision ended without a name being given to me or any other details and shortly thereafter, the plane landed in New York and we were enroute to the host hotel.

I had been invited by one of the host ministry leaders for the event to attend a joint Board meeting of the organizations co-hosting and sponsoring the Prayer Summit, and it was a small intimate dinner meeting of around 20 leaders in a luxurious, spacious, high rise conference room. When I arrived a few minutes early for the dinner, my host graciously introduced me to the other attendees, and to my shock and amazement, one of them was the man I had seen in the vision earlier that day on the airplane. His name was Graham Power and he was from Capetown, South Africa. Mr. Power is Chairman of the Power Group of companies and also founder and Chairman of The Global Day of Prayer.

After I was introduced to him and we exchanged pleasantries, I told Graham that I had received a vision for him and asked if he would like for me to share it. He immediately took a digital recorder from his pocket and asked me to share what I had seen. As I shared the vision and its interpretation, the tangible glory of God and anointing of the Holy Spirit rested on and around us, and we both strongly sensed God's pleasure and presence. Graham thanked me for being obedient and for sharing this confirming word, we exchanged business cards, hugged each other, and a few minutes later the dinner started. Had I not been obedient to the leading of the Lord, I would have missed this important and strategic assignment. Truly God is touching the nations through the prophetic, since the Global Day of Prayer was birthed through a vision that the Holy Spirit gave Graham in July 2000, and a decade later (in 2010) all 220 nations of the Earth were represented.

One final intercession story that I feel lead to share is from a trip that I was part of several years ago to LaPaz, Bolivia and Lake Titicaca, which lies half in Peru and half in Bolivia. Bolivia is among the poorest nations on the earth, and in both Peru and Bolivia, the Philippines, India, Brazil, and many other places on earth, children live on garbage dumps. This trip was sponsored by Fullness in Christ Ministries, led by Ras and Bev Robinson. On this particular trip, led by Apostle David Newsome, Temple, Tex. and his wife Prophet Petie Newsome, our mission was to meet and minister to local leaders, set up rice evangelism programs for several churches and orphanages in the regions, purchase initial food supplies, conduct evangelistic services as well as street evangelism, and conduct strategic intercession. As a result, a number of people came to know the Lord and received salvation.

One of the more interesting aspects of this trip was the opportunity to be involved in strategic intercession and to prophesy to local and regional leaders. Did I mention that LaPaz has the highest altitude of any airport in the world? The altitude definitely takes a little getting used to. One sunny day we interceded outside the presidential palace, the legislative headquarters building, the vice president's office, a large Catholic church, and the three largest banks in Bolivia. All of these were located within a few blocks of each other. Then on another day, which was overcast and raining, our team was driven to a mountain overlooking Lake Titicaca, which was several hours from La Paz by car. Lake Titicaca is considered by many experts to be one of the most potent centers of black magic in the world. Many priests come from Tibet, India, Nepal and other nations to renew their black magic powers at Lake Titicaca. There is even rumored to be one or more demonic idols buried deep in the lake, and there is an ancient temple ruins nearby.

Our team was told by an indigenous apostle who seemed well-informed that as part of the last presidential inauguration, a baby boy was cut in seven pieces and his body sent to different parts of the nation by one of the spiritual advisors to the president. We were not able to verify that, but instead had to pray for a short while inside our vehicle after arriving at the mountain for the rain to stop so we could carry out our assignment that day, and after 30 minutes, the rain stopped only where we were parked and on top of the mountain, and kept raining everywhere else in sight.

After reaching the summit after a brisk 30 minute nearly vertical hike, we discovered a demonic altar and tore that down and performed several land repentance acts and ceremonies over several hours, built an altar to the Lord, and made a number of decrees over Peru and Bolivia. As we were finishing, the rain began again and before we could start down the mountain, one of our team members began to experience symptoms of hypothermia due to the coolness of the altitude. The team leader and I bundled her up with gloves and extra jackets and hustled her down the mountain and into a waiting warmed car in time to prevent any problems. After a visit to a restaurant on the lake, a delicious and inexpensive fish and vegetable lunch, and a few prayers and prophetic acts over the lake, we called it a day and returned to our hotel. I am fully expecting those decrees to have an effect and to come to pass.

Perhaps the highlight of this trip, however, was a visit to the downtown marketplace in La Paz one night. We were in search of a group of street kids known to get high from sniffing glue. After some effort we found a group of them and offered to buy them dinner from a street vendor. With some hesitation they accepted and we watched them eat several plates of food. As they were eating, the Holy Spirit spoke to me about one young woman and said, "She is ready to come into the Kingdom." So I asked her if she would like to receive Jesus as her Lord and Savior. She said, "Yes!" and our team began praying for her. After a few moments, the rest of the group came over and said they wanted the same thing. The entire group of street kids received salvation through a word of knowledge and the gift of Prophetic Evangelism.

So, over the last six to seven years I have come to understand and appreciate the power and importance of Prophetic Intercession. Anyone who is doing or attempting to do something significant for God and His Kingdom needs a Prophetic Intercession team. A phone call from an intercessor with a word from God confirmed the location of the first K.E.Y.S. event in 2008. His exact words were, "God said to tell you that this first K.E.Y.S. event is to be held at PromiseLand Church in Austin rather than a hotel." That short phone call saved me a lot of time and hundreds of thousands of dollars. Interestingly, I had just met one of the pastors of that church a few months earlier when I had convened and led an intercession meeting on a Saturday at a hotel in Austin in obedience to a word from the Lord. There was a strong anointing there and around 65 people attended from across Texas. When Pastor Charlie from PromiseLand left that day, he had said, "If you ever want to hold another meeting in the city, let me know." So God confirmed His plan for the event. Other subsequent words have confirmed other strategic details.

I have also served on or lead three intercession teams for two other ministries and a corporation during the last several years and I have a lot of interesting stories and lessons I could share from that experience. For two of these groups, I lead a stealth team of prophetic intercessors that provided spiritual screening and discernment for potential job applicants, recruits, and new hires, and potential strategic partners. Our group was below the radar screen and so technically did not exist, similar to a special operations or "black ops" team. I interfaced with senior management only as needed. Many amazing testimonies have resulted from these activities but those must remain confidential for a number of reasons.

Prophetic discretion in particular, and ministerial discretion in general, are important to God. The old adage, "Loose lips sink ships," is true. Not everything that we see or hear or that God shares with us is meant to be shared publicly. So, with the gift, mantle, unction or office, we need wisdom and discretion also. God needs to know that He can trust you with sensitive or classified information in the spirit realm. Some things God shares only on a need to know basis, and with those He trusts.

This concludes our study of Prophetic Intercession. In the next chapter we will look at Prophetic Activation.

You will also
declare a thing,
And it will be
established for you;
So light will shine on
your ways.
Job 22:28 NKJV

Chapter Seven

Prophetic Activation

S ometimes with prophecy, something leaps on the inside of you or comes alive. The baby in Elizabeth's womb leaped when Mary, pregnant with Jesus, entered the room and spoke (Luke 1:41-44). On the road to Emmaus, the two men who had been with Jesus asked themselves, *"Did not our hearts burn within us as we talked with him?"* (Luke 24:32). Sometimes a prophetic word resonates with our spirit to such a degree that ignition or activation or detonation occurs in our spirit man. This can also happen as a person reads the Holy Scriptures. An internal shift happens, something new is birthed, or something comes alive on the inside of us.

Just as there are so-called "trigger events," there are also "trigger words." A particular passage, phrase or word can suddenly come alive or quicken in a person's spirit as fresh revelation and understanding come flooding in. The word made alive, or the spoken word, is called *rhema*, in contrast to the written word, called *logos*. Different things that can be activated by the prophetic include creativity, spiritual gifts, identity, destiny, acceleration, healing, finances, employment, conception, spiritual climate, political climate, etc.

An iron axe head dropped in a river floated to the surface at Elisha's word (2 Kings 6:1-7). Rain fell at another prophet's word, and ceased at yet another word. A prophet once outran a horse and chariot at a distance of almost 20 miles. Elijah called down fire from heaven on more than one occasion to deadly effect. An entire city (Nineveh) repented at one prophet's message (Jonah). A dead man came back to life when his body came in contact with Elisha's bones (2 Kings 13:21). Elisha once cursed in the name of the Lord a group of insolent young mockers who called him "thou bald head," or in today's terms, "baldy," and two she-bears came out of the woods and tore 42 of them. Are you getting the picture yet?

Sometimes a prophecy activates a person; at other times the word catalyzes a group, region or nation. The prophet is one of the governmental offices in the church. The Bible says in the New Testament that the apostles and prophets are the foundation of the church, as we have discussed previously. There is a lot of authority and responsibility that comes with being a prophet. God increases that and God promotes you as you are faithful. The Scripture says, *"He that is faithful in the little will be ruler over much"* and it also says that *"promotion comes from the Lord."*

> Sometimes a prophecy activates a person; at other times the word catalyzes a group, region or nation.

Some people in ministry and business are self-promoters. They promote themselves in different ways. Some try to get honorary degrees or online diploma mill degrees or Bible school degrees from non-accredited institutions and call themselves "Doctor." They name drop, they join prestigious groups, they attend the right conferences and join the right associations, and pull strings and leverage connections. There are many other ways that people try to self-promote. Sometimes they try to bypass and shortcut the processes of God. When they do that, it ends in disaster because they are not ready for what they are trying to do and they are not really prepared either for promotion. They have not produced the requisite maturity and character, and they have not paid the price for what they want to walk in and the deeper things of God.

Yes, God has an order. God has a process. So, the idea of Prophetic Activation is like the story in the New Testament, when the baby in Elizabeth's womb leaped when Mary entered the room. Mary was pregnant with Jesus at that time. All she came to do was visit her cousin who was pregnant with John the Baptist.

In his book entitled *The Dimension of Sound*, Dr. G.E. Bradshaw describes a powerful revelation of the account of Luke 1:39-42 (KJV):

> *"And Mary arose in those days, and went into the hill country with haste, into a city of Judea, and entered into the house of Zacharias, and saluted Elisabeth. And it came to pass, that, when Elisabeth heard the salutation of Mary, the babe leaped in her womb, and Elisabeth was filled with the Holy Ghost: and she spake out with a loud voice, and said, Blessed art thou among women, and blessed is the fruit of thy womb."*

The word **salutation** is from the Greek term *"aspasmos,"* meaning: A greeting in person or by letter. (Strong's) The term *aspasmos* contains the word *spasm*, meaning: An involuntary and abnormal muscular contraction. When Mary spoke, it released a contraction of both Elisabeth's natural and spiritual wombs. The baby leaped in her womb and she began to prophetically proclaim the plan of God for Mary's life! The term **leaped** is from the Greek word *Skirtao*, meaning: To sympathetically move (as the quickening of a fetus) (Strong's).

Scripture says that the baby in Elizabeth's womb **leaped** and so a lot of times when I am ministering prophetically, I never know when that is going to happen. Sometimes when I share a word, I might be giving someone a 30 minute prophecy, and there might be one word in that prophecy, or one phrase or one sentence, that when I speak that, the word(s) triggers something on the inside of the person's spirit and it is like a detonation word or a trigger word that sets off a chain reaction inside their spirit.

That person might start manifesting the presence of God and fall out in the Spirit. They might start jumping up and down. They might start screaming or yelling in joy, hope, comfort or agreement, and being overjoyed. They might start laughing hysterically, crying or running around the room. All I know is that the prophetic carries with it a dimension of activation that's very different from any of the other four five-fold gifts or offices mentioned in Scripture. So, there is a special property with prophecy and the prophetic of being able to activate things in people's spirits.

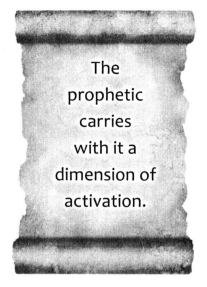

The prophetic carries with it a dimension of activation.

There is even a creative aspect to activation. Prophets can activate a female's womb. I have seen prophets praying over women that were barren and unable to bear children or men whose sperm count was too low and the dimension of prophecy in the way that it worked was able to supernaturally cause fertility and conception to happen in that person's womb. There are many testimonies like that throughout church history. For example, Drs. Mahesh and Bonnie Chavda have seen many examples of that in their ministry.

Prophecy has the effect and the ability to cause something to come alive on the inside of us. Sometimes you can be struggling. You can be stuck somewhere and when you receive a prophetic word, it has an encouraging property about it, but it can go way beyond encouragement to actually be life producing. It can be life giving to your spirit and if you grab hold of that, then it can accelerate and activate what God is doing. Those are a few thoughts about it.

The word I would add to that is *Rhema*, which means "it's the word that is quickened or comes alive." When you are reading the Bible sometimes a word or phrase or passage of Scripture will seem to jump off of the page, a new revelation or insight will suddenly come forth, or you will see or understand something that you might have missed previously. Similarly, you can be receiving a prophecy from someone and half of what they are saying you may not understand or it may not be impacting you. But, when they get to the part of the prophecy where your spirit is sucking that word in because your spirit is so dry and thirsty and so hungry for what is being spoken over you, then that is the Rhema word that is quickened and comes alive inside of you.

This concludes our discussion of Prophetic Activation. In the next chapter we will explore Prophetic Portfolios.

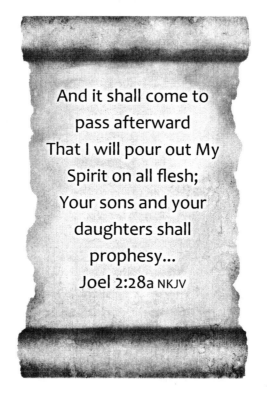

And it shall come to
pass afterward
That I will pour out My
Spirit on all flesh;
Your sons and your
daughters shall
prophesy...
Joel 2:28a NKJV

Chapter Eight

Prophetic Portfolios

What I mean by the term "Prophetic Portfolio" is that God has given each of us a portfolio just like in the business world or investment community where you may have a basket of businesses and/or investments, either that you manage or where you are a passive owner. You may have some micro stocks, you may have some penny stocks, commodities, fixed income, real estate, distressed debt, and/or gold and silver in your portfolio. In business, you may own a franchise, or you may own or be part of several different income-generating enterprises. That is certainly optimal and financially healthy as we read in Ecclesiastes 11:2, *"Invest in **seven ventures,** yes, in **eight,** for you do not know what disaster may come upon the land"* (NIV, author's emphasis).

In fact, there is a specialized branch of study in academia in finance known as portfolio theory, where you can study portfolio selection, portfolio modeling, portfolio management, portfolio forecasting and portfolio allocation, among other things. Previously

I worked for a private asset management company overseeing a large university system endowment where I helped to manage and invest billions of dollars, so I have witnessed and participated in this principle being demonstrated in the marketplace.

This is the same concept with a Prophetic Portfolio, which is your different mantles or expressions of the gift that God has given you in the realm of the prophetic. Jesus had a five-fold portfolio which included the prophetic and apostolic as well as teaching, evangelizing, and pastoring. His portfolio included healing the sick, raising the dead, preaching the good news of the Kingdom, doing what He saw the Father in heaven doing, casting out demons, setting the captives and prisoners free, binding up the broken-hearted, discipling a few trustworthy men, and generally destroying the works of the devil (Isa. 61:1-2, Luke 4:18-19; Mark 16:15-18).

> Prophetic portfolios are different anointings or mantles you carry in the prophetic.

I will also use myself as an example to illustrate this concept. God has given me several areas of gifting and authority in the prophetic dimension. Prophetic Portfolios are different anointings or mantles you carry in the prophetic—your different gift mixes, assignments and how you flow and operate in the prophetic. For me, these include inner healing and deliverance, land repentance, writing, song of the Lord, fathering, branding, seer gift, activation, third heaven experiences, marketplace (business, finance, economics), wealth transfer and spiritual experiences (angels with scrolls, etc).

He has given me a grace for inner healing and deliverance — the ability to pray for people and use the prophetic gift to see the root cause of why they are stuck or why they have trauma or wounds that they received sometime in the past. Another part of my Prophetic Portfolio is that I have learned through inner healing and deliverance with people, that these same principles apply to dirt, and apply not only to raw land but improved land. I have seen these principles work on condominiums, apartments and office buildings, and also oil leases. I have seen some amazing miracles through this process.

Then the third part of my Prophetic Portfolio is songwriting and prophetic songs using the prophetic in worship and music. I have been involved in recording or producing four different CDs and my wife and I have co-written two of them by recording and arranging what the Holy Spirit was downloading to us at the time. I am getting this revelation today as I am writing from the Holy Spirit. It is something that I went to the Lord and asked Him to supply. I simply asked the Lord to download His title for the book and His chapter outlines and content and He did.

I would say for Prophetic Portfolios, it is like branding; I was a marketing director for 12 years in a prior season of my life, and God is really into naming things. Names have significance in the Kingdom. So, now in my business consultant practice, the Lord will give me brand names for clients. I would say "Lord, what is your name for this business? Or, what is your name for this product?" and as I listen, the Holy Spirit just tells me and every time I get the name for a business or a product for my clients directly from the Holy Spirit. When I check the domain name (URL) of whatever I have heard, it is always available at that time: the .com, .net or .org are still there. The trademark is always available. It is a valuable gift for business consultants to have this prophetic grace.

Then I would say that another part of my Prophetic Portfolio is activation. The Lord has given me a gift of activation whereby I pray for people and see a dormant gift or gifts that they had not realized were there or that had not been activated in them be imparted or activated. This obviously produces a new level of faith in them. I also have a gift of faith, a father's heart and fathering mantle. That is a part of my Prophetic Portfolio as well.

Then I have a mantle for finance and business and I am able to pray and prophesy for people and break the spirits of bankruptcy, lack and poverty; pray for blocking, eliminating and canceling debts; and pray for supernatural release for wealth transfer for people to move into different dimensions of business. I also have an acrostic or acronym anointing whereby I hear things for people around the beginning letters of their first and last names. It has been uncanny over the years the detailed information I have received about people just from their name. I stopped trying to figure it out a long time ago and just accepted and flowed with it.

Part of my Prophetic Portfolio is Celestial Prophecy where I have had encounters with angels and with scrolls and third heaven experiences in different rooms and places in heaven. So, it is different with each person. But, it is important to inventory yourself and be aware of your Prophetic Portfolio so that you will know what issues you will have authority over when different situations come up and different opportunities present themselves.

Another aspect of one's Prophetic Portfolio deals with language and dialect. The level of a person's vocabulary, their skill in description, the accent of their language and their temperament in delivery of words all lend to the type of demonstration they portray when they prophesy. People often expect a completely different vocal delivery under the prophetic anointing than one has with normal speech or conversations. In reality, God uses who you already are and what you already have in you to demonstrate his power and purpose. This is why it is important to constantly enhance your portfolio by reading and studying the Bible and other books and materials related to prophetic ministry. Even newspapers, magazines and business manuals lend to the total language library of people who prophesy. What you have stored in your memory banks becomes a great part of your prophetic arsenal.

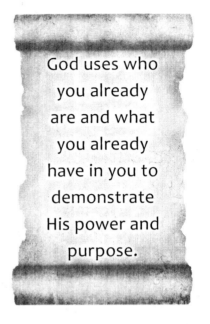

God uses who you already are and what you already have in you to demonstrate His power and purpose.

John 14:26 shows how memory plays a role in the prophetic. *"But the comforter, which is the Holy Ghost, whom the Father will send in my name, he shall teach you all things, and bring all things to your remembrance, whatsoever I have said unto you."* (KJV) The term *remembrance* is taken from the Greek word *hupomimnesko*, meaning — to remind quietly, to suggest to the memory or to put in one's mind (Strong's). This means that the Spirit of the Lord can cause us to recall information previously learned as a vocabulary file from which to draw the language of the prophetic or to reveal words that were learned previously but had been forgotten. However, God is not restricted to this and can reveal totally new words or phrases that we have never known, simply because He is God. People who have limited vocabularies generally prophesy within the limits of their vocabularies, so we need to be open to learning. In our next chapter, we will look at Prophetic Testing.

For we know in part
and we prophesy in
part. But when that
which is perfect has
come, then that
which is in part will be
done away.
1 Cor. 13:9-10 NKJV

Chapter Nine

Prophetic Testing

P salm 105:18-19 says, *"They hurt his feet with fetters, He was laid in irons. **Until the time that his word came to pass, the word of the LORD tested him"*** (NKJV, *emphasis added*). The NIV translation says in verse 19, *"till what he foretold came to pass, **till the word of the Lord proved him true"*** (author's emphasis).

This Scripture has intrigued me for many years. The idea that the prophetic word Joseph had received in a dream as a teenager **tested** him for 13 long years in a foreign land is a profound one with implications and applications for us today. The first and second use of *word* here is *Imrah,* meaning: Commandment, speech or word. The word "tested" here is the Hebrew word *Tsaraph,* meaning: To fuse or refine as by a metalsmith (Strong's). So, literally the word of the Lord to Joseph tested him in the same way that metalsmiths remove impurities from metal by refining processes, typically involving extreme heat, and that blacksmiths forge swords and other metal objects to strengthen and harden them so the metal does not break or fail under pressure or in battle.

Many of you have been, are being, or will be tested (as Joseph was) by the word of the Lord that you have received through prophecy. The greater the prophecy or prophecies you have, the greater the testing will be. Just look at the life of Jesus as an example of that principle. Hebrews 2:10 says that Jesus was made perfect through the things He suffered. You and I will be, too.

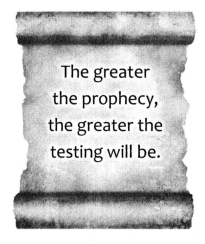

The greater the prophecy, the greater the testing will be.

Now that I am a little older and wiser, I am not so quick or eager to run after other prophets in hopes of receiving a prophetic word. First of all, the Holy Spirit can speak to me directly; secondly, I have many prophets in my inner circle; and thirdly, I have learned that whenever I receive a powerful prophecy that seems impossible or beyond me, invariably I must go through a process before the word is fulfilled, such that more testing and character and maturity will be required of me to walk out that word and see it come to pass in my life. This process produces death in my flesh—including any carnal or worldly thoughts, mindsets or habits I may have in a particular area—and life in my spirit man, and in my renewed or regenerated mind. Once I have passed the test and mastered the lesson or skills God needed me to learn, graduation and promotion naturally follow, although on God's timetable and in God's way.

Joseph had to endure 13 years of testing and that is about the equivalent of becoming a medical doctor today. Joseph had to get through undergraduate school in being sold into slavery by his brothers and serving Potiphar and being tested and falsely accused by Potiphar's wife. He had to go through graduate school by going into the prison as an innocent man. Then he did his doctorate or postdoc for two years while stuck in the prison after the wine steward was released and went back to serve Pharaoh on the royal court. God tested him and the vision, the dream and the Word that Joseph had that was in his heart; he was tested to see if he was worthy and ready for that Word to come to pass and if he was able to handle the Word.

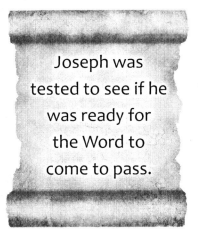

Joseph was tested to see if he was ready for the Word to come to pass.

We are not told why Joseph had to wait in prison another two years after he interpreted the dream of Pharaoh's cup bearer (wine steward) three days before his release and restoration. It may be that God had Joseph in finishing school, continuing to chisel and shape and hone or fine-tune his character and deepen his prayer life and intimacy with the Lord. It may be that Joseph ministered to others in prison during that time who needed his godly counsel and wisdom. It may be that the cupbearer was busy with his renewed responsibilities, and simply forgot Joseph. Or, it may be that the cup bearer was too embarrassed to mention the name of a slave in Pharaoh's court. And possibly, God was preparing Pharaoh for what was to come and working on his heart. It is important to mention this possibility, because often our destinies and our prophecies affect and involve other people. And, just because we are ready, it doesn't mean they are. God's purposes and plans tend to be revealed in the fullness of time (see Rom. 5:6).

A lot of people get Words and the reason it may take 10 or 20 years for that Word to come to pass is that they do not have the character or maturity to handle that Word. Or, it may be that their prophecy is linked to or involves someone else's destiny as well. If that Word would have been fulfilled the next day, it might have destroyed them. They would not have had a clue what to do with it. So, God is not going to give us more than what we can handle or more than what we are ready for, or than He has planned or purposed for us.

We also need to distinguish between the words "tempt" and "test." Although God tests His children, He does not tempt anyone. James 1:13-14 says, *"When tempted, no one should say, 'God is tempting me.' For God cannot be tempted by evil, nor does he tempt anyone; but each person is tempted when they are dragged away by their own evil desire and enticed."* One of the ways God tests us is through the prophecies we receive. Abraham and Sarah were tested by prophecy on several occasions. Abraham wavered not through unbelief, but considered that God was able to fulfill all that He had promised; because of this, he is called the father of faith.

What I have learned and experienced in my own life and in seeing the lives of others that I have prophesied over, is that the greater the word, or the greater the prophecy, the more testing will be involved in that prophecy, and the more process will be involved for that prophecy to come to pass. When I was younger in the prophetic, I just ran to any kind of prophet that was available or came to town. I had the time to go and hear the prophet. I would just attend the meeting hoping to get another prophetic word or confirmation.

I have matured past that now so I am not looking for that any longer. Now the prophecy is finding me through my circle of friends and my network and/or by just hearing from God directly, when I am journaling or praying or reading the Bible or even through dreams when I am asleep on my bed. God speaks to me through dreams sometimes. So, I am no longer chasing prophecy. Now, prophecy is chasing me. I think that is a much more healthy and balanced approach to the prophetic and what God prefers for us.

So, this is what I mean by Prophetic Testing. Abraham and Sarah were examples. They were tested by prophecy. The Lord said that they would have have a child in their old age. Scripture says that Sarah laughed about it and at first Abraham questioned the promise because they were beyond childbearing age. Sarah chose to "help" God along (since she was too old) and gave her servant Hagar to Abraham as a concubine. They created a huge problem with Ishmael that is still plaguing the Middle East today. Ishmael had 12 sons just as Jacob did. That should be a warning to us to avoid creating Ishmaels with our prophecies.

So, these are things that are inferred by the idea of Prophetic Testing. When you receive a Word from God it does not mean that it will automatically be fulfilled unless there is a covenant, oath or causation involved on God's part. What it usually means is that there is a process that will be involved in walking that Word out, and part of that process will likely involve testing over some period of time. Testing helps to prepare us for our divine assignments and destinies. Next we will look at the subject of Prophetic Patterns.

Follow the way
of love and eagerly
desire gifts of
the Spirit, especially
prophecy.
1 Cor. 14:1 NIV

Chapter Ten

Prophetic Patterns

I included this chapter to encourage people not to treat or consider their prophecies in isolation, but to look at them in total—as a whole—to gain more clarity and insight. Begin by looking for themes and patterns in prophecy, not just words and images. Look for tapestries, connections, threads, etc. Learn to see the patterns and themes in your prophecies. Record your prophecies and transcribe your prophecies. Then pray over them and agree with them, and share them with those who have spiritual oversight or authority in your life. Look for the bigger picture of what God is doing in your life and has called you to be and do. Learn to differentiate between assignment(s), identity, purpose and destiny in your life.

When I was a graduate student and doctoral candidate at the University of Texas at Austin, I had to choose between qualitative and quantitative research methodology for my dissertation. After weighing the pros and cons of each, I chose qualitative research as my primary methodology and grounded theory as my research protocol. Briefly, grounded theory is theory constructed through a multi-stage process of open coding, axial coding, and selective coding of the data for a particular qualitative study. It is concerned respectively with identifying conceptual categories, dimensions and properties of the categories, and relationships between the categories. According to Strauss & Corbin:

> A grounded theory is one that is inductively derived from the study of the phenomenon it represents. That is, it is discovered, developed, and provisionally verified through systematic data collection and analysis of data pertaining to that phenomenon. Therefore, data collection, analysis and theory stand in reciprocal relationship with each other. One does not begin with a theory, then prove it. Rather, one begins with an area of study and what is relevant to that area is allowed to emerge (p. 23). Strauss, A. & Corbin, J. (1990). *Basics of Qualitative Research: Grounded Theory Procedures and Techniques.* Newbury Park, CA: Sage.

In grounded theory, you look for themes or concepts and you use tools like data mining, triangulation and coding. You are looking for how things connect. You are looking for how things are confirmed from different directions and dimensions. I used descriptive analysis and triangulation in my national study to uncover the key themes of my research topic and to develop a theoretical model of fundraising effectiveness for predictive purposes, and to identify the key elements and variables of that model. Similarly, whenever I read through the numerous personal prophecies I have received over the years, I see patterns and themes emerge.

This rigorous academic program that I completed was excellent training and gave me a frame of reference for understanding prophecy and the prophetic. Allowing the data to speak for themselves in research rather than beginning with a theory and then trying to prove it, has powerful spiritual analogy and application for the prophetic. It means that we don't judge a person by outward appearances or circumstances but look beyond the flesh and the natural into the spiritual dimension and into the person's heart. Of course, such academic training is not required for God to use you in prophetic ministry, which is more about the heart than the head. But, God will use whatever tools you give Him to work with.

Sharnael Wolverton says in her book, *Keys to Third Heaven* (2007, p. 129), that the conventional "See and Say" approach to prophecy is not always the best one available in every situation. According to her: "Sometimes we are only to *See and Pray*. Mostly we are to *Dig and Decree!* The higher prophetic calling is to be a treasure finder." That is so true! Looking beyond the issues and problems or challenges in the people, churches, cities, companies or nations we prophesy to and seeing the potential, seeing the future, seeing the hidden or buried treasure that God sees in them, and uncovering or bringing that forth through the prophetic, is essential to building up the body into the image and maturity of Christ. I thank God that I have pastors and other leaders who did that for me, who saw the treasure and potential buried inside me and invested themselves in my life and in my growth and development. Without that, we fall short of God's best in ministry.

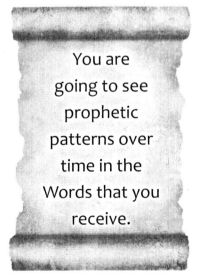

You are going to see prophetic patterns over time in the Words that you receive.

Prophetic Patterns develop over time as God weaves a tapestry in your life. By Prophetic Patterns what I am saying is I personally have received in my own life from other people around a thousand prophetic words over the last 19 years. I haven't counted them and don't ever plan to, so I don't know the exact number; it might be 500, it might be 1000 to or it might be 1500. I am pretty sure it is at least 1000 at this point. What I do is I record and transcribe them and when I have the time, every few months or so, I just read through some of them and pray. By doing that, what I see is there are particular themes in my prophecies. I see that there are patterns of how God speaks to me.

With Prophetic Patterns, everything usually reverts back to the original purpose for which God gave the prophecy. Patterns and purposes are business partners in the prophetic. Patterns will always support God's purposes and God's purposes will always support patterns. The only way to truly reproduce and perfect something is to see the pattern and purpose that it represents.

Patterns and purposes are business partners in the prophetic.

As minute as some prophetic words may seem to be, they are always part of a bigger picture and will eventually lend themselves to the synergy of God's individual words that people receive over the course of their lives. Isaiah 28:10 tells us *"For precept must be upon precept, precept upon precept; line upon line, line upon line; here a little, and there a little."* (KJV) Every part adds up to form the total plan that God desires. This is why it is important to document our prophecies, and also to be vulnerable when we prophesy. I have learned that the things I see and hear for people which seem to be the least important and most insignificant, often have the most impact or meaning for the person. As you compare words that you have received, you will begin to see the patterns that show you the synergy and scope of God's movement and plan in your life.

In almost every prophecy, there are going to be particular themes and patterns that God is communicating through the prophecy. For me the most frequent prophetic words that I have received personally have to do with nations, wealth transfer, Kingdom finance and financial infrastructure, Josephs, leadership, Israel, the marketplace, fathering, the five-fold, building bridges and being a connector and a conduit for the body of Christ, and things related to that. These are my Prophetic Patterns, and are the basic themes that I see in my personal prophecies repeatedly.

Even in writing this book, as an example, I received prophecies for two years from at least a dozen prophets that God wanted me to write books on the Kingdom, so this was on my spiritual radar screen, but I had not yet received a timing and release. In faith I made out a moderate-sized list of possible topics and book titles, and waited on the Lord. The prophecies I had received kept saying "now" but in the natural I didn't see how this was possible due to my other time and financial commitments. Finally, the Spirit spoke to me directly and said, "Begin writing on Thanksgiving Day 2010 and rearrange your schedule for the next few months because this is a priority." So, that night I sat down and began receiving revelation and the structure and outline and words for this book and ideas began flowing and have not stopped. It was divine timing and divine order. I had not planned to write this book first, and in fact had already written half of another book, but God had other plans.

Part of having your prophetic words established is that if this is something really important, and is something God wants you to do, He is probably going to give you the same prophetic word multiple times in several different ways from at least two or three different people. Over time you are going to have major themes in your life and in your destiny from your prophecies. You are going to see Prophetic Patterns over time in the Words that you receive. God says in His Word that important things should be established at the mouth of two or three witnesses. So, look for your prophetic themes and patterns to better understand your spiritual identity, assignments and destiny.

This concludes our discussion of Prophetic Patterns. In the next chapter we will look at the seven levels or dimensions of the prophetic.

Seven Levels or Dimensions of the *Prophetic*

There are different levels and dimensions of prophetic ministry, and it is important to recognize and distinguish between them. This chapter will explore and explain the differences and distinctions between these seven levels and dimensions.

1) Prophetic Non-Awareness

Prophetic Non-Awareness is the first level or dimension of the prophetic. This is where some of the church, and much of the nonChristian world, currently finds itself. Most often we see this expressed in dreams. Because it is natural and healthy for us to dream nightly, God often speaks to us in dreams. Job 33:14-18 states, *"For God does speak—now one way, now another—though man may not perceive it. In a dream, in a vision of the night, when deep sleep falls on men as they slumber in their beds, he may speak in their ears and terrify them with warnings, to turn man from* *wrongdoing and keep him from pride, to preserve his soul from the pit, his life from perishing by the sword"* (NIV, *emphasis added*). This Scripture says that God is speaking to man in different ways, but that man may not perceive or be aware of it. In other words, men may not recognize the voice of God or may not be tuned to the frequency of heaven. Five different purposes are listed for God's dream communications with man.

Another verse that reinforces this lack of prophetic awareness by mankind is found in Gen. 28:10-22. As Jacob was fleeing from his brother Esau, and heading toward his relative Laban's abode in Paran, he stopped and spent the night enroute and used a stone for a pillow. He had a dream in which he saw a stairway reaching from earth to heaven, and angels ascending and descending on it. There above it stood the Lord, and God spoke blessings, protection, increase and generational fruitfulness over Jacob, and promised to bring him back to his homeland someday.

Verses 16-17 read, *"When Jacob awoke from his sleep, he thought,* **'Surely the Lord is in this place, and I was not aware of it.'** *He was afraid and said, 'How awesome is this place! This is none other than the house of God; this is the gate of heaven.'"* So, he took the stone he had slept on, set it up as a pillar, and anointed it with oil, and named the place Bethel ("house of God"). The Hebrew word for **gate** is *sha'ar*, which means: an opening, i.e., door or gate. The Hebrew word for **heaven** is *shamayim*, which means to be lofty; the sky (Strong's). Many people don't realize that God has opened the gate from heaven to earth through the death, burial and resurrection of Jesus, and the release and baptism of the Holy Spirit.

Similarly, prophets and apostles open the gates over churches, cities, regions and nations. So, these two barriers and challenges of perception and awareness speak of man's need to hear from God, the fact that this is not natural except for those born of the Spirit, and the need to become intentional about knowing God and training our senses, including the spiritual eyes and ears of our heart, to become sensitive and attuned to God's voice and presence. The good news is that in both examples God was speaking to man. He is still speaking today and it is our responsibility to train our spiritual senses and cultivate an intimate relationship with God.

2) Prophetic Unbelief or Counterfeits

Some in the church and many in the world are currently at this second level or dimension of the prophetic, where they have heard of prophecy and are aware of it, but either 1) don't believe in it; or 2) don't believe that it exists or applies today or has applied since the last of the original twelve apostles died or the last chapter of the Bible was written; or 3) in the case of the world, many practice or engage in counterfeit prophetic forms such as New Age, mediums, psychics, occult, or false prophets from other religions. The fruit produced from such spirits is very different than the true spiritual fruits of the Spirit of God. For a more in depth discussion of Counterfeit Prophecy, read the section in Chapter Twelve.

Prophecy for some people is like a "paranamoral phenomenon." They acknowledge its existence but don't understand what it is, where it comes from, how it works, or what its true nature and purpose is. This book was written to help remedy that.

3) Prophetic Spirit

A marketplace loss often leads us to the prophetic. Saul got more than he bargained for. He recovered his fathers' donkeys, but in the process, he received a prophetic destiny from Samuel, and his spirit was changed into that of another man. That is the effect the prophetic anointing has upon people when they visit a prophetic house, church, center, company of prophets, school of prophets, etc. There are prophetic ministries with such a strong anointing or mantle on them that visitors to their services who have never prophesied before are sometimes moved to prophesy or see visions.

I Samuel 19:20-24 is a great example of the **Prophetic Spirit** in action. King Saul sent a battalion of soldiers to capture David, and instead the soldiers began prophesying and apparently were incapacitated and unable to carry out their orders and assignment due to the effects, including intensity and duration, of the Prophetic Spirit. In fact, that same spirit then came upon Saul and he lay down and prophesied naked all night at the feet of Samuel.

A measure of wisdom and grace is required to properly administer the prophetic gift.

The best example of a Prophetic Spirit is in the Old Testament before Saul became the first King of Israel and his father had lost some of the donkeys that belonged to the family business. So, his father sent Saul and a servant on a mission to find the lost donkeys. As Saul was traveling with the servant and they were going to different nearby cities looking for their lost family donkeys, he came upon the prophet Samuel. Samuel told him, *"You need to go in this direction. There you will find your donkeys."* He gave certain direction.

Saul encountered a group of prophets along the way and most theologians believe that it was a school of prophets. Saul approached this group of prophets as he was looking for his lost donkeys. Scripture said that the spirit of God fell upon Saul and he was changed and became a different man and began to prophesy.

This happened several times in Saul's life — even later after he became king this happened. This is what I call the Prophetic Spirit and this is what happened with me.

When I first began to receive the gift and grace of prophesying, I visited the church that I was a part of for the last eleven years where I served as an elder. The very first time that I set foot in this particular church, in His house, I began to have visions. I had never had visions before. I had never prophesied before, but there was a Prophetic Spirit over this particular church. It was so strong that when I just came in contact or even came in to the physical church building, it activated something that was inside of me that God had deposited. But, it took a certain spirit and the right timing of God for that prophetic gift to be released and activated in me.

This is the Prophetic Spirit and what happens is sometimes people can visit a church that is highly prophetic or strongly prophetic and people who have never prophesied before, never had visions before, occasionally one day will visit a church that is known to have this gift in great measure and abundance. The spirit in that house or on that church will sometimes affect the person so that they will begin to prophesy for the first time. A Prophetic Spirit can also affect a region, as in the case of Maria Woodworth-Etter.

4) Prophetic Gift

The gift of prophecy (**Prophetic Gift**) is the third level or dimension of prophecy, and is given by Jesus through the Holy Spirit to individual Christians. Individuals can choose whether to cultivate and develop and use their gift or not. They can also choose whether to pursue training in the prophetic, attend prophetic conferences, seek out a prophetic mentor, read books on prophecy, be part of a church where prophecy is taught, practiced and embraced, etc. Promotion and rewards come from the Lord in things of the Spirit.

We are stewards of the spiritual gifts God has chosen to give us. We should work as unto the Lord and not unto man in all that we do and say. We should want to hear these words spoken to us by Jesus: *"Well done, good and faithful servant."*

In 1 Corinthians 12 there is a gift of prophecy listed as one of the nine gifts that Jesus gave to the church through the Holy Spirit. So, the Prophetic Gift is available to all persons. Jesus desires that people will have the gift of prophecy and this would be where you actually receive what I would call a "spiritual grace" because gifts are all free and all given from God as He wills.

If you receive a Prophetic Gift, that means that God has graced your life or imparted a special measure of grace to hear Him and see into the Spirit realm. And, really to operate as a prophet, there are several different parts to that; it is not just hearing the voice of God, it is not just seeing into the spirit realm and seeing the hearts of people, seeing future events, seeing visions and trances and having third heaven visitations. But, it actually includes interpreting and understanding what you are seeing and the timing of that.

It is also the gift of wisdom in knowing how to filter what you see. For example, if you are in a public setting and see a vision of a person committing adultery or some other type of sin, you may want to share that with the person privately rather than publicly. There is a measure of wisdom and grace that is required to properly administer the Prophetic Gift.

5) Prophetic Mantle

The next level or dimension would be the **Prophetic Mantle**. The best example in Scripture is when Elijah was walking past Elisha who was out in the field plowing with the 12 yokes of oxen. Elijah threw his mantle onto Elisha. Now Elisha knew what that meant.

When a spiritual leader or prophet would throw their mantle on you, it was an invitation to come and serve them, to come and be discipled by them, to come and be mentored by them. Elisha told the prophet Elijah, *"Well, just give me a few minutes and I will say goodbye to my parents."*

So, he killed one of the yoke of oxen and had a great feast and barbeque and said a proper farewell to his parents and then left everything he was doing and followed Elijah. And, he served Elijah for some period of time; scholars believe it was between 12 and 20 years or somewhere in that range. There was a season when he was really under the mantle or the covering of a senior prophet, someone who was already well established and well seasoned in the things of God.

I have done this for other prophets. Several prophets over the years have asked me to mentor them prophetically and teach them about the ways of a prophet and to help them in nurturing and maturing their gifts. Also this goes with taking them to meetings, and ministering publicly or privately with these junior prophets that you are mentoring. This would be the phase I would call the Prophetic Mantle phase — when you are developing a gift and deepening a relationship with God and maturing as a person and as a leader and serving, and you are coming into the fullness of what God has for you.

6) Prophetic Unction or Presence

The word "unction" has several meanings, one of which is smearing, rubbing, or anointing. During the course of writing this book, several senior prophets have shared that they differentiate between prophesying from the gift of prophecy and prophesying from the presence of God. Among those are Dr. Gordon Bradshaw and Stacey Campbell. I also can notice and discern the difference between prophesying out of the gift versus prophesying out of the unction or presence. According to Campbell, in her book *Ecstatic Prophecy*, "What happens to me when I prophesy can be put into two categories: prophesying out of the gift and prophesying out of the presence of God. Sometimes I may begin by prophesying out of the spiritual gift of prophecy, which I can activate at will. When I, out of my own will, activate the resident gift I experience no physical manifestations. Often, however, in the middle of prophesying out of the gift I can feel the Spirit of prophecy, or the presence of God, at a tangible level" (2008, p. 84).

Some prophets tend to experience the presence of God in predictable patterns. Some, like Campbell, shake involuntarily. Others don't. In the three-to-four-hour encounter I had with Jesus in early 1995, I received a powerful "wave anointing," and had the sensation of being gravity free and floating in an ocean of God's love with giant 100-foot waves of energy crashing over me repeatedly for several hours. This was the same type of encounter that Charles Finney experienced and described in his journal.

Something about that encounter changed my "hard wiring" on the inside—like going from 110 to 220 volts. Ever since then, when I pray for people or lay hands on them, often they feel a wave anointing. So, there is something to be said for the reality of spiritual imprinting, although I experience God in many different ways and forms and on many different levels. Like Campbell, I can feel when the presence of God is on me or around me, but I can typically control physical manifestations such as shaking, although sometimes they are more pronounced, but rarely involuntary. If that happens, I will usually sit down in a chair to continue prophesying.

7) Prophetic Function or Office

Those who serve in the function or office of a prophet are recognized by fellow prophets and apostles as being seasoned, mature, and trustworthy with the things of the Spirit — able to handle the word of God accurately, rightly dividing the Word of truth, rightly discerning spirits, and being steadfast and instant in season and out of season. These are stewards of the gift who have exercised and trained themselves to hear and see and communicate the words and visions of God accurately and effectively. These trusted stewards of the prophetic often have words for nations and for cities and people groups, and at times warn of impending natural disasters and other calamities, including God's judgments.

The office of the prophet is really what is listed in Ephesians and 1 Corinthians in the New Testament where it is talking about the five-fold. In this list are the teacher, the pastor, the apostle, the evangelist and the prophet. These are the five-fold graces or callings or offices in the body of Christ, and this is a special measure of the prophetic. It goes beyond being a gift because people who are senior and mature, who are established and recognized and accepted in the gift of prophecy, over time, it is possible for them to come into the office of the prophet, which is the place of widespread acceptance and recognition and honor in the body of Christ and greater authority and wisdom and trustworthiness.

So, the *metron* (measure of rule or sphere of authority) of the office of the prophet goes beyond giving individual prophecies or being a local prophesier or body prophesier or just giving prophecies to different churches or different denominations or just roaming around as an itinerant prophet and giving personal prophecies to people. These are prophets that are writing books, serving as senior counselors, teaching or leading schools, giving prophetic words to nations, and shifting the economy or culture or government of cities, regions and/or nations through their prophetic words and visions and acts. These are prophets that are counseling presidents and heads of states and corporate titans of industry and mentoring and discipling other younger prophets, and warning of impending disasters or seasons and windows of opportunity.

Technically the word "office" is not used in the Bible and so I believe a brief discussion of this concept and term is in order to establish the biblical basis for its use here.

By "office" we mean position or function in reference to the five-fold ministry. Eph. 4:11 says "...*He has appointed...*" (AMP). So first, we must differentiate between elected office and appointed office as regards the five-fold ministry. Since Jesus gives or distributes these gifts to whomever He chooses, these are appointed positions or functions and cannot be elected at will by the ambitious and/or upwardly mobile or more aggressive Type A personalities among the body of Christ. Many people claiming these titles are self-appointed and are easy to spot and discern because their ministry reeks of flesh and self and lacks noticeably the power, presence and fruit of the Spirit and the favor of God. God said about Paul the Apostle, "*He is my chosen vessel.*" So, God chose him and appointed him for a specific work and task.

God calls and commissions, but man ordains. Some people may never be ordained whom God has called and commissioned. So, in things of the Spirit, titles are not always helpful and can be misleading, although they do have some value and benefit. We have to look instead at position or function as well as character. There are at least three types of authority that can come into play and should be discussed with each of the five-fold offices or functions—

positional authority (leading and leveraging other leaders), functional authority (how well we function in the particular five-fold grace God has called us to), and relational authority (how well we serve others and relate to them and lead by example). Although Jesus exhibited all three types of authority, He only rarely used positional authority and almost always used functional or relational authority. That is a model we should follow today in five-fold ministry and in leadership.

A word that is similar in meaning to **appointed** is **set**. 1 Cor. 12:18 says, *"But now hath God set the members every one of them in the body, as it hath pleased him"* (KJV). The Greek word for **set** in this passage is **tithemi**, which means "to place." So, God has placed each of us in the body of Christ where it most pleases Him. This same word is also used in 1 Cor. 12:28, *"And God hath set some in the church, first apostles, secondarily prophets, ..."* (NIV).

1 Cor. 4:9 says, *"For I think that God hath set forth us the apostles last..."* The Greek word for **set** in this Scripture is **apodeiknumi**, which means to show off, exhibit, prove, set forth. Finally, in Hebrews 2:7 we read, *"For thou madest him [man] a little lower than the angels; thou crownedst him with glory and honour, and didst set him over the work of thy hands"* (KJV). The Greek word used here for **set** is **kathistemi**, which means to place down (permanently), to designate, constitute, convoy, appoint (Strong's). So, these verses teach us that God was very intentional about placing prophets in the prophetic function in the church; in fact, prophet is the only one of the five-fold gifts or offices listed which was carried over from the Old Testament.

There are **Body Prophets** (assigned to a local church, group of churches, or a denomination), **Itinerant Prophets** (who travel and minister anywhere they are invited or the Lord sends them),

Teaching Prophets, and **Senior Prophets**—fathering prophets, mentoring prophets, and patriarchal prophets like Bob Jones, Bishop Dr. Bill Hamon, Dick Mills, John Sandford, and others. There are also matriarchal prophets like Patricia King, Anna Mendez Ferrell, Cindy Jacobs, Sharon Billins, Stacey Campbell, Michelle Seidler, Barbara Wentroble, Beth Alves, Tommi Femrite, Sandie Freed, Jane Hamon, Peggy Cole, and Gwen Shaw. Bob Hartley was apparently referred to by God as a "patriarchal prophet" in a recent third heaven experience he had with Jesus, so age is apparently not as much a criteria as experience and intimacy and spiritual maturity.

In a prophecy released in the 4th quarter of 2010, Hartley stated, "It is needed and necessary for the Family of God to hear in the year to come from a **true patriarchal prophetic** that always has an answer in Him! In the past, the prophetic has magnified the issues above our "Greater than" God. Each one of us is being invited into this process individually as God leads, to come out with an answer in Him and be unmoved."

Hartley added: "Jesus said he is talking to me as one who is a father that really cares and nurtures and stewards the lives of others with the words He gives, and He said, 'I have entrusted you and others with this word to be not only a tutor but a father, with the heart of the **hopeful patriarchal prophetic** who long to see their sons and daughters go even farther than them in who I am and their authority and dominion in Me, as fathers and mothers who can decree a thing and it happens.' They were given hearts of flesh with such love, it will change the prophetic movement and I saw them come like trees that were so tall with heavenly food for all the earth to eat from, like Psalm 1 and Isaiah 61.'"

In summary, these are seven of the different levels or dimensions of prophetic reality, expression, or maturity. Now we shall explore the twelve types or classes of prophecy in the next chapter.

Twelve Types or Classes of Prophecy

The Holy Spirit has shown me that there are at least 12 types or classes of prophecy, and is now releasing me to share this revelation and write this book. It is designed both for the body of Christ and for those who are attracted to things of the Spirit but not yet born again. I did not include Creative Prophecy as a separate class, because I believe that all prophecy is creative. Likewise, I did not include Catalytic Prophecy as a separate class, because I believe that all prophecy has life and power and force. Job 22:28 says, *"Thou shalt also decree a thing, and it shall be established unto thee: and the light shall shine upon thy ways."* (KJV) Likewise, Isaiah 55:11 says, *"So shall my word be that goeth forth out of my mouth: it shall not return unto me void, but it shall accomplish that which I please, and it shall prosper in the thing whereto I sent it."*

1) Causal Prophecy

The first among the twelve types or classes of prophecy is **Causal Prophecy.** Causal or **Causative Prophecy** would be prophesying from the First Cause. We know from Physics that God is the First Cause of the universe. When He said, *"Let there be light"* — that is a Causal Prophecy. When He created man and said, *"Let them be created in our image"* — that is Causal Prophecy. That is when the Lord directly speaks something into existence, or temporarily overrides physical laws of the universe.

The first few chapters of Genesis record a number of such Causal prophecies, as does Job 38:1-42:6, which records God's creation in great detail. When Jesus said, *"Lazarus come forth,"* that was a Causal Prophecy. In the Old Testament, God caused the sun to move backward on the sundial for King Hezekiah in response to the prophet Isaiah's prayer (2 Kings 20:8-11), and for the sun to stand still and the moon to stop for an entire day for Joshua in response to his prophetic decree during battle (Joshua 10:12-14).

2) Covenantal Prophecy

The second type of prophecy is **Covenantal Prophecy.** Certain individuals stand out. God established covenants with certain individuals such as Noah, Abraham, Moses and David. Sometimes God seals covenants with a prophecy or forms a covenant through prophecy. Sometimes an oath is also involved with a covenant. God made a covenant with Moses, and with Israel, in Exodus 34:10-28. God continued this covenant with Joshua after the death of Moses (Joshua 1:1-9). There are at least three references to covenants in the life of Abraham (Gen. 12:3, 18:18, 22:18). God said your seed will be as the sand of the oceans on the seashores; then He said your seed will be like the stars of the heavens. He also told Abraham that he would have a child in his old age. God established all these prophecies with covenant and oath (Heb. 6:13-15).

He did the same thing with Noah. The story of Noah may be the most dramatic example of Covenantal Prophecy. When God destroyed the world by a great flood, he preserved a righteous remnant in the form of Noah's family, in addition to the various animal species, through the provision of an ark which Noah and his family built according to God's instruction and blueprint or pattern. With Noah, He established a sign which was the rainbow. He said, *"I will never destroy the earth by water or flood again."* That was a Covenantal Prophecy that God made with mankind and with Noah. He said it as He sealed this prophecy with a visible sign that we can still see today with a rainbow. This is a physical symbol of a spiritual reality, and a continual confirmation and reminder of this oath or covenant.

Then with King David, God said, *"David, you will never fail to have a man from your seed on my throne forever."* In this covenant or oath that He made to David, He fulfilled that Covenantal Prophecy through Jesus Christ coming through the line of David (Acts 2:29-31). Isaiah 9:6-7 also talks about the government or *basilea* of God being on the shoulders of Jesus and him reigning on David's throne. Jesus has an eternal priesthood in heaven after the Order of Melchizedek, according to Hebrews Chapter 7. Jesus also sat down at the right hand of God after his ascension, and is the firstborn of many brethren, and the Second Adam. Therefore, David's lineage has an eternal throne established in the heavens and God's oath or covenant with David was fulfilled.

3) Communal Prophecy

The third type is **Communal Prophecy** or **Community Prophecy.** These are prophecies to a people group or to a city or state or nation or a local church, but in all cases they are given to or intended for a group of people rather than an individual. One such example of Communal prophecies would be the Prophet Daniel and all the Old Testament prophets as well because they were primarily charged with prophesying to Israel — either the entire nation of Israel or the divided kingdom, depending on which time period the prophet lived in. That was the particular people group, the Jews, that God raised up and commissioned and called specific prophets to speak to that *ethnos*.

Daniel was the prime minister or chief administrator (satrap) during five different monarchs or rulers in the Medio-Persian Empire. Communal Prophecy speaks to not just an individual or not just in general but to a specific group, city, state, region or nation.

Daniel's prophecy to Belshazzar in Daniel 5:26-28 is one example. *"God has numbered the days of your reign and brought it to an end...Your kingdom is divided and given to the Medes and Persians."* In Daniel 7:1-28, Daniel had a dream of four animals or beasts which symbolized four future kingdoms on the earth. Another such example is Ezekiel's vision of the Valley of Dry Bones and the resulting vast army which formed and assembled after he prophesied in Ezekiel Chapter 37.

Many of the Old Testament prophets were called and assigned to prophesy to the nation of Israel or the Jewish people. Their calling, destiny and purpose was linked primarily to one culture and one government (see Ezek. 3:5-6, Isa. 6:1-13, the entire book of Hosea), etc. Jonah had a different call to other people groups (Jonah 1:1-2), as did Jeremiah (Jer. 1:1-10), whose call was to the nations. Jeremiah

1:5c says "*I appointed you as a prophet to the nations.*" Then verse 10 says, "*See, today I appoint you over nations and kingdoms to uproot and tear down, to destroy and overthrow, to build and to plant.*" There are prophets today with similar callings and assignments for specific nations or continents. In the New Testament, Peter and Paul each had different primary assignments to people groups— one to the Jews and one to the Gentiles—although each ministered a bit to both.

4) Commercial Prophecy

The fourth type is **Commercial Prophecy**. Commercial Prophecy is prophecy that is directed in the marketplace, in business, or in finance. When Jesus told Peter to go and take the coin from a fish's mouth and to pay his tax and Jesus' tax — that was a Commercial Prophecy.

One of the best examples is the story of Laban and Jacob where Laban had been cheating Jacob out of his wages for about 10 years as he was attending Laban's flocks. God gave Jacob a vision and in this vision he actually saw the different animals, the herds and the sheep coming together at the watering trough. He saw these rods in the water and some of the sheep were speckled and some were spotted. Such animals were considered in those days as inferior.

He made this business plan based on the vision he saw from God which was a type of Commercial Prophecy. He actually made a bargain and renegotiated the contract with His employer, Laban, and said, "*From now on you just give me the worst of your herds and flocks. Just give me the new offspring of the speckled or the spotted and then you keep all the normal animals.*" Laban readily agreed to this proposal which seemed so greatly weighted in his favor. God used that to greatly increase the wealth of Jacob and actually made him wealthier than Laban. There was a wealth transfer that happened through that vision over a period of about 10 years.

God spoke to Isaac in Genesis 26 and told him to plant. That verse says, *"Isaac planted in the time of famine and reaped a hundred fold in the same year."* Amazing! In one year, Isaac's obedience to God's word produced a hundred fold return in a time of famine, where a lot of people around him were suffering. This is an example of the effect of Commercial Prophecy on the body of Christ.

On one occasion Paul was beaten, jailed and whipped for harming the commerce of Demetrius the Silversmith and his peers (Acts 19:23-41). On another occasion, when Paul cast a demon out of a young woman diviner, her handlers realized that they had lost their means of income, and they became angry and filed false charges and stirred up trouble for Paul and Silas and had them beaten and thrown into prison (Acts 16:16-40). Preaching, prophesying, and casting out demons have the potential and power to change the economies of neighborhoods, cities, counties, states, provinces, regions, and nations.

My friend Johnny Enlow, a speaker, prophet and author, once prophesied in Peru the existence of an undiscovered silver mine, salt mine and zinc mine, and a lost ancient city (La Gran Saposoa) within 100 miles of the particular city he was visiting (San Martin). He said he thinks this was in 1999. Within 18 months, he said all of these were discovered and since then, both mining and tourism revenues have increased dramatically, and the economy and unemployment rate of the entire region were positively affected. Johnny said this region formerly had the nickname "the cancer of Peru" because two different guerilla groups were based in the province, and drug crops (coca) were grown there, but now the district has been transformed and is known as "the fruitbasket of Peru." Johnny also prophesied the existence of an undiscovered large gold mine near Trujillo, Peru, and said that also was discovered soon afterward and is among the largest deposits and active mines in Peru.

Perhaps the most famous account of Commercial Prophecy is in Luke Chapter 5, verses 1-11, where Jesus told Peter to *"Let down the nets"* after he had fished all night and caught nothing. The result was sudden and supernatural. Scripture says, *"When they had done so, they caught such a large number of fish that their nets began to break. So they signaled their partners in the other boat to come and help them, and they came and filled both boats so full that they began to sink."* (NIV) The fishermen were amazed and astonished, put their boats in storage, and followed Jesus.

A later account in John 21:1-14 after Jesus' resurrection mentions a catch of 153 fish after Jesus told the disciples to throw the net on the right side of the boat. These were not small fish, as they completely filled the net, and the writer found it remarkable that the nets did not break, so it is possible that the disciples made enough money from this one event to be able to provide for their families while they followed Jesus.

On a personal level, the Holy Spirit speaks to me in business on a regular basis. Several years ago, the Lord spoke to me and told me to repent for my closed-minded attitude toward real estate investing. I immediately repented and two weeks later an individual I had recently met at a business executive luncheon called and asked me to join him for lunch at his country club. At the lunch, he presented a real estate development project to me and asked me to arrange the financing for it. I told him I would pray about it and would get back to him within a few weeks. On the drive home, the Lord spoke to me and told me that this opportunity was part of my inheritance from Him. My wife agreed with me in prayer about this opportunity, and so we moved forward with the project. The initial round of financing of $3.7 million came together and closed in just over 45 days. Now I own part of the development.

About a year later the Lord spoke to me and said, "I want to give you another income stream." Soon after that, I was presented with an opportunity in a new network marketing company owned by several Kingdom-minded individuals in my city. I was a bit skeptical since I had never been involved in that industry before on a serious level. After performing due diligence and trying the nutritional products for several months, getting to know the management team, and learning the compensation plan, I made a commitment to join and God has blessed this decision.

A business friend of mine once contacted me to let me know he was losing $30,000 a month in debt service on a $3M condominium project. The construction was brand new and ready for occupancy, and even with an ideal location, the building had attracted no tenants. I told my friend I would meet him on location the following Saturday morning and when I arrived we began to prayer walk the property. The Lord told me to go to the third floor to a certain room and once inside the room, the Lord showed me a vision of a dead body lying in a pool of blood. I told my friend that I would meet him the next week with a team of intercessors and we would deal with the demonic spirits on the premises. The next Saturday, after an hour and a half of spiritual cleansing and land repentance, we discerned that the demonic spirits had left the property. Within two weeks the building was 50% occupied and was fully occupied within six weeks and remains so at the time of this writing.

Several years ago I had earned some stock warrants from consulting services I provided for a technology company. I exercised the warrants for around $750. After four years the CEO of the company called me one day and made me an offer to buy my shares of stock. I sought counsel from a pastor and several prophets at my church on whether or not to sell the stock at the price offered. The Holy Spirit spoke through these men and unanimously told me I should sell the stock and that if I held it, the value would plummet. I sold the stock immediately for a nice profit and several months later the company closed its largest revenue-producing division, significantly decreasing the value of the shares and the profitability of the company.

Jesus wants us to walk on the water like He did, and that involves both faith and risk. God wants to show us how big His plans and ideas for us are but we have to ask Him, and then listen and obey. He is the God of both the more than enough and the impossible. (Luke 1:37)

5) Celestial Prophecy

Celestial Prophecy is prophecy where you are caught up into the heavenly realms. These are Celestial prophecies or Revelation that prophets receive when their spirits are having a third heaven visitation, when they are actually "caught up" or taken into the dimension of the heavens where God's throne is and God is directly speaking to their spirit man, as in the case of apostle John, where he not only heard things from God, but he saw things in the future and in the heavenly dimension — some of which they were able to share in the case of John and some of which they were not able to share as in the case of apostle Paul.

A modern-day example of this is Pastor Jesse Duplantis. He had an experience where he was taken up into the heavenlies several years ago. He has written a book about it. He has explained it and testified about what he saw there on television. Many people currently are having these type of experiences. It is not just limited to apostles and prophets today, although they are the primary candidates, but others sometimes have these type of celestial experiences as well. Children have been known to experience this.

Some prophecies result from or occur while in a trance state, while having a vision, while conversing with angels, or while being caught up into the third heaven realm. This chapter will focus on this latter class of prophetic experience although we will reference one particular trance. The best examples of this in the New Testament are with the apostles Paul, Peter and John. In some cases, the person having such an experience is not able to discern in what form the experience is taking place, *"whether in the body or out of the body"* (in the Spirit). In other words, the person having this type of divine experience and seeing things in a different dimension is not always able to discern whether their spirit man is having this experience apart from the body or whether their natural (physical) man is also involved.

Paul the Apostle had at least one such third heaven encounter that he shared in 2 Cor. 12:1-4, in which he was *"caught up to the third heaven."* The Greek term *harpazo* means "caught up." *Harpazo* literally means "To seize, pluck, pull, take up by force." *Tritos* is the Greek word for "third," meaning: a third part. The number 3 also represents wholeness, fullness or completion. *Ouranos* is the Greek word for "heaven," meaning: to rise or elevate, heaven as the abode of God, the sky, happiness, power or eternity (Strong's).

This eloquent and educated apostle who wrote much of the New Testament also had a direct supernatural encounter with Jesus (while still named Saul) on the road to Damascus, in which he fell to the ground and was blinded for three days after Jesus spoke to him (Acts 9:1-9). God had to speak to Ananias in a vision to get his attention, and then had to convince him that his mission was necessary and important. Note in this passage that God had already spoken to Saul in a vision and he had seen Ananias praying for him before Ananias even arrived (v. 12). Sometimes people have already seen us in their future, and are waiting for us and expecting us, and we are still arguing with God about going to minister to them. Note that Jesus told Ananias that Saul was his "chosen instrument" or "chosen vessel" or "personal representative" (v.15). This is why prophets cannot judge by the outer appearance, but must learn to see the heart of a person, and discern their spiritual identity and destiny. God qualifies the call rather than calling the qualified, and a person's current appearance or circumstances may not reveal their status or potential in God's plan and Kingdom.

John the Apostle also had a third heaven experience as recorded in Revelation, beginning in Chapter 1:10, in which he was "in the Spirit" on the Lord's Day, meaning, in a state of spiritual ecstasy. *Pneuma* is the Greek word for "Spirit." "*Immediately I was in the Spirit; and behold, a throne set in Heaven, and One sat on the throne.*" Revelation 4:1-2 says, "*After these things I looked, and behold, a door standing open in Heaven. And the first voice, which I heard was like a trumpet speaking with me, saying, 'Come up here, and I will show you things which must take place after this.'*" *Thura* is the Greek word for "Door," meaning: The opening or closure to a portal. *Anabaino* is the Greek word for "Come up," meaning: To ascend, arise or spring up (Strong's).

Peter the Apostle in Acts 10:9-16 was praying on a roof at midday in Joppa and fell into a trance. Verse 11 says that "*He saw heaven opened.*" The word for "Opened" in Greek is *anoigo*, from "*Ana*" meaning: upward, severally, in, through, repetition, intensity and reversal; and "*Oigo*," meaning: to open up (Strong's).

The prophet Ezekiel in the Old Testament also had a similar experience where "*the heavens were opened*" (Ezek. 1:1) and he saw visions of God in the third heaven realm. The Hebrew word for "opened" is *pathach*, meaning: to open wide, to loosen, begin, plow, break forth, draw out, unstop and vent (Strong's). The gateway to the heavens was enlarged and became visible so as to provide the ability to plow through, break yokes, draw out, unstop and vent the places that were previously restricted. New resources were made available because the view from heaven's perspective was now visible.

Once when I was teaching a prophetic training class, I was praying for a woman who was blindfolded to be able to see in the spirit and for God to activate her prophetic gift and spiritual senses. As I was praying for her, I suddenly found myself in an unknown room with four walls, a floor and a ceiling, and there were rows and rows of masks of different designs and colors that covered every square inch of the four walls. From memory, there were at least hundreds of masks in the room, and perhaps thousands. I sensed that I was in a training room in heaven called the Mask Room. Immediately I felt the presence of Jesus in the room and I heard Jesus ask, "Which mask am I behind?" I sensed a particular one and said, "That one, Lord." Jesus answered, "You have seen well. Teach my prophets that they must look beyond the exterior and the outward appearance, and see behind the masks people wear, and gaze with the eye of the Spirit into the hearts and souls and spirits of people."

In closing this section, I think it appropriate to mention the amazing third heaven experiences of the children at the Baker School and Adullam Orphanage/Rescue Mission operated by Harold A. and Josephine Baker in Kotchiu, China in Yunan Province. The Bakers wrote a book about their experiences titled *Visions Beyond The Veil,* describing their lives and experiences from the early 1900's to 1949, when they were forced to flee to

Hong Kong when the Communists took over China. These were the grandparents of Rolland Baker, who with his wife Heidi, oversee Iris Ministries in Mozambique.

6) Corrective Prophecy

Then another type is **Corrective Prophecy**. There are many types of Corrective prophecies mentioned in the Bible. Corrective Prophecy is when God uses a prophet to deliver a message, either a warning message like you may get a warning ticket from the highway patrolman for speeding, but if you are driving erroneously, the ticket will be the actual fine. Sometimes God will use a prophet to deliver a judgment as He did with Nathan in the case of David. Nathan went to see David after he had committed adultery with Bathsheba and she became pregnant with David's child and her husband Uriah the Hittite had been killed in battle because of David's instructions to his military commander Joab to withdraw from Uriah while in battle. Nathan told David a story about a wealthy shepherd who stole his poor neighbor's only sheep. He said, *"David, what should happen to such a man"*? And David became angry and said, *"Well, he shall repay fourfold for it."*

God allowed David to pronounce His own judgment and during the rest of David's life, four of his children met untimely or violent deaths, and that prophecy was fulfilled out of the mouth of David through Nathan the prophet. There are other examples like that where prophet Samuel gave Corrective Prophecy to King Saul in 1 Sam. 13:13-14 and announced that the Kingdom had been removed from him and his house because of his sin in offering a priestly sacrifice. *"You have acted foolishly and your kingdom will not endure,"* Samuel told him. *"The Lord has sought out a man after his own heart and appointed him leader of his people."* Although it took many years for Saul and his son Jonathan to die in battle with the Philistines, followed by the assassination of his son Ishbosheth, the prophecy did come to pass, and David succeeded them as king.

Jonah gave a Corrective Prophecy of judgment to the City of Nineveh and the Assyrian people, and his words had a sobering and transformative effect on the king and his people. Jonah 3:4 says that Jonah came into the outer part of the city on the first day and prophesied that the city would be overturned (destroyed) in 40 days. All of the Ninevites believed God, declared a fast, and put on sackcloth. When the king heard about this, he joined them. Then the king and nobles issued a decree in which they said in part, *"Let everyone call urgently on God. Let them give up their evil ways and their violence. Who knows? God may yet relent and with compassion turn from his fierce anger so that we will not perish."* (Jonah 3:8-9) Then verse 10 says, *"When God saw what they did and how they turned from their evil ways, he had compassion and did not bring upon them the destruction he had threatened."*

Among the more dramatic and interesting examples of this type is the story of the rebellion of Korah, great-grandson of Levi, and his 250 followers who were members of the council, along with On, son of Peleth, and Dathan and Abiram, the sons of Eliab. Apparently these men coveted the priestly position and functions of Aaron. In Numbers 16:28-30, Moses prophesied as follows: *"This is how you will know that the Lord has sent me to do all these things and that it was not my idea. If these men die a natural death and experience only what usually happens to men, then the Lord has not sent me. But if the Lord brings about something totally new, and the earth opens its mouth and swallows them, with everything that belongs to them, and they go down alive into the grave, then you will know that these men have treated the Lord with contempt"* (NIV).

Verses 31-33 state, "*As soon as he finished saying all this, the ground under them split apart and the earth opened its mouth and swallowed them, with their households and all Korah's men and all their possessions. They went down alive into the grave, with everything they owned; the earth closed over them, and they perished and were gone from the community.*" Verse 35 adds, "*And fire came out from the Lord and consumed the 250 men who were offering the incense*" (NIV). So, the Lord confirmed the leadership of Moses and Aaron before the congregation and ended the rebellion, though not until another 14,700 Israelites were killed by a plague.

In the New Testament, a somewhat different yet equally dramatic event took place to confirm the leadership of the apostles. A couple named Ananias and Sapphira sold a piece of property and came and laid part of the money at the apostles' feet. Peter said to him in Acts 5:4, "*You have not lied to men but to God.*" Acts 5:5 says, "*When Ananias heard this, he fell down and died.*" Three hours later his wife came in and also lied to the apostles about the price of the land. Peter prophesied in Acts 5:9, "*Look! The feet of the men who buried your husband are at the door, and they will carry you out also.*" Verse 10 says, "*At that moment she fell down at his feet and died.*" So, these are some examples of Corrective Prophecy in the Bible.

7) Conditional Prophecy

The next type is **Conditional Prophecy**. Conditional Prophecy is basically prophecy that relates to human nature, free will and obedience, rather than to things like world events, historical facts, laws of physics or the plan of God. This class is neither Causal nor Covenantal Prophecy. Instead, there is often an if-then component, and the recipient of this kind of prophecy must believe it, and add both faith and "feet" to it. Nik Wallenda, who amazed and inspired the world on June 15, 2012 by becoming the first person to walk across Niagara Falls on a tightrope, said, "I was born for this," and that he had trained his whole life for that one feat. He also said that he felt God's presence with him.

I would say that the majority of prophecy today is probably Conditional Prophecy because that is where the person receiving the prophecy actually plays a part in it by their response to it, by their level of faith and obedience, as to whether their prophecy is ever actually fulfilled or how long it takes to fulfill the prophecy. The Bible says, "*According to your faith, so be it done unto you.*" The Bible also says that Jesus Christ is the same yesterday, today and forever, and that God is not a man that he should lie. God is also not a respecter of persons. Therefore, any issues with nonperformance or nonfulfillment of prophecies are not on God's side of the table— they are on ours.

An example of Conditional Prophecy is when Jesus told the rich young ruler to go and sell all that he had and distribute it to the poor, and then come and follow Jesus so that he might have eternal life. Scripture says the ruler went away sorrowfully. Jesus outlined the conditions necessary or required for him to have eternal life, and the man refused them and turned his back on Jesus. That's why personal prophecy is often specific and highly individualistic, because God knows our hearts, and our motives and character. Another example of Conditional Prophecy is when Jesus told some of the disciples, "*Come and follow me and I will make you fishers of men.*" The conditions were following and discipling. The disciples had free will and could have refused. But, as Peter said once, "*Where shall we go Lord? You have the words of eternal life.*"

8) Carnal Prophecy

The next type is **Carnal Prophecy.** 1 Cor. 3:1-4, 7-8 and Rom. 7:14 talk about the carnal man. Carnality refers to our flesh on the earth. Carnal Prophecy is prophecy where there is a mixture of spirit and flesh. Often, there is a lying spirit involved like in the example of the Old Testament and the Prophet Micaiah who prophesied against Ahab that he would die in a particular battle (1 Kings 22:17-23; 2 Chron. 18:16-22).

Even though 400 other prophets in the king's service had prophesied that Ahab would be victorious in this battle, Micaiah gave a famous word where He said (paraphrased), *"God was seeking counsel from the spirits of wisdom in His court and around His throne as to how to induce you to attack this city so He could kill you, Ahab. The best way for that to happen was to send a lying spirit into your prophets."* One of the 400 false prophets was highly insulted by that prophecy and went and slapped Micaiah in the face. As Micaiah was being led away to prison for giving that word, he shouted to Ahab, *"If you ever return safely, the Lord has not spoken through me."* Ahab was killed very soon afterward when he went into the battle in disguise.

Sometimes you might hear or receive prophecies that violate history or violate facts or violate laws of physics that could not possibly be true. What that tells you is that sometimes you have to "eat the meat and spit out the bones" in prophecy from less mature and unseasoned prophets — people who are beginning in their journey and getting comfortable with the gift or mantle; that is why you need to get discernment and confirmation with prophecy. Some people give so-called "pizza prophecies" or "parking lot prophecies." The implication with both is that flesh or immaturity is involved or that accepted protocol is absent.

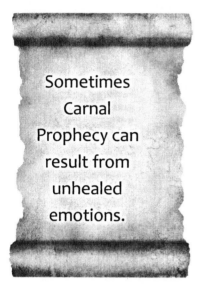

Sometimes Carnal Prophecy can result from unhealed emotions.

Sometimes Carnal Prophecy can result from unhealed emotions, as when a word is given with unrighteous anger, and prophets project their own unhealed pain, trauma, rejection or other issues in the words they give. Rejection is common to all prophets, but some master it and others are mastered by it. Those who carry unhealed rejection often give harsh and condemning and judgmental prophetic words. Not surprisingly, most of those people are not under spiritual covering or spiritual authority or accountability because they have not learned to trust or relate to a spiritual father or mother or be part of a team. Their unhealed rejection and wounds create more rejection and wounds, and this is a vicious cycle that is self-defeating and self-sabotaging for them.

Other Scriptures which reference lying prophets or false prophets include 1 John 4:1, Jer. 14:14, Ezek. 13:3-9, 2 Pet. 2:1, and Matt. 7:15-16. Several of these Scriptures are particularly harsh. Jeremiah states, *"Then the Lord said to me, 'The prophets are prophesying falsehood in my name. I have not sent them nor appointed them nor spoken to them; they are prophesying to you false visions, divinations, idolatries, and the delusions of their own minds'"* (NIV). That is strong language. But, it gets even stronger.

Ezekiel records, *"God, the Master, pronounces doom on the **empty-headed prophets** who do their own thing and know nothing of what's going on! Your prophets, Israel, are like jackals scavenging through the ruins. They haven't lifted a finger to repair the defenses of the city and have risked nothing to help Israel stand on God's Day of Judgment. All* they do is fantasize **comforting illusions** and preach **lying sermons.** They say 'God says...' when God hasn't so much as breathed in their direction. And yet they stand around thinking that something they said is going to happen. Haven't you fantasized **sheer nonsense?** Aren't your sermons tissues of lies, saying 'God says...' when I've done nothing of the kind? Therefore—and this is the Message of God, the Master, remember—**I'm dead set against** prophets who substitute illusions for visions and use sermons to tell lies. I'm going to **ban** them from the council of my people, **remove** them from membership in Israel, and **outlaw** them from the land of Israel. Then you'll realize that I am God, the Master" (MSG, author's emphasis).

Matthew 7: 15-16 says, "*Watch out for false prophets. They come to you in sheep's clothing, but inwardly they are ferocious wolves. By their fruit you will recognize them.*" I have encountered a few of these ferocious wolves claiming to be prophets, and they are indeed a dangerous and predatory breed. One such wolf coaxed, cajoled, and coerced contributions totalling a large sum of money from a single elderly woman by gaining her trust and confidence through a prophetic gift, and then preying upon her emotions during a time of life-threatening illness by promising that God would heal her if she would donate to his ministry. This left her and her family financially destitute, and the woman and her family could no longer make their mortgage payments and were soon forced to forfeit the title of their spacious home and move into much smaller accommodations. This is just one example among many which could be cited.

According to Matt. 7:21-23, on the Day of Judgment some will say to Jesus, "*Have we not prophesied in your name and cast out demons and worked many miracles?*" And he will reply, "*I never knew you. Away from me, you evildoers.*" So, clearly, being a prophet or a deliverance minister or a miracle worker does not guarantee you eternal life. Basically then, Carnal Prophecy spans the spectrum from immature prophecy to false (non) prophecy.

9) Catastrophic Prophecy

The ninth type is **Catastrophic Prophecy** or **Warning Prophecy**. This class includes prophecies that foretell natural disasters such as floods, fires, earthquakes, illness or death, terrorist attacks, etc. There may be some overlap here with the earlier section on Corrective Prophecy, such as the case of Jonah prophesying judgment on the city of Nineveh. But, there is enough distinction in my opinion to warrant a separate discussion and attention.

Several years ago when Hurricane Katrina hit land there were a number of prophecies released. The same thing happened with the 2008 election campaign, and both before and after the terrorist attack on the Twin Towers in New York on 9-11-01. Representative prophets who have given accurate prophecies related to such events include Kim Clement, John Mark Poole, Dr. Chuck Pierce, David Wilkerson, John Paul Jackson, Cindy Jacobs, Bob Jones, Rick Joyner, Terry Bennett, etc. (this is by no means an exhaustive list). But, just because a prophet sees destruction or a disaster or catastrophe in a dream or vision, does not mean that such things will actually come to pass (see Jonah 3:10). So, the primary intent of such prophecies is warning—as a precursor to either Judgment, Repentance or Preparation.

Many dreams or visions involve disasters or catastrophe, and some of these are natural disasters, while others are man-made disasters. The prophets, intercessors and watchers/watchmen are part of God's early warning system in the Spirit realm.

10) Calendar Prophecy

The tenth class is **Calendar Prophecy**. An example of a Calendar Prophecy is famous dates in history, or anniversary dates. The Jewish calendar is obviously devoted to and heavily focused on feasts and major religious holidays. There is a certain day in Jewish history that is feared more than other days because disaster has happened repeatedly on that day, the 9th of Av (Tisha B'Av), over the centuries for the Jews. Likewise, the Feast of Purim is a celebration of the Jews exacting revenge on their enemies and plundering them. This feast originated during the reign of Queen Esther but has been celebrated ever since. And some of the prophecies, visions and dreams Daniel received, as discussed earlier in the section on Communal Prophecy, could be considered Calendar prophecies because they have timelines attached to them (days and weeks). Much of eschatology involves a study of current events and Scriptural timelines.

Cindy and Mike Jacobs traveled to Wittenberg, Germany a few years ago after the Lord spoke to them and they visited the famous Wittenberg Cathedral where Martin Luther had posted his 95 Theses 400 years earlier on Oct. 31. Cindy used revelation gained from that experience and others to write a book on *The Reformation Manifesto*. First Bob Jones and more recently (since 1996) Bobby Conner have issued a Sheherd's Rod newsletter each year around the time of the Jewish new year, Yom Kippur. Bob Jones in particular has issued several prophecies related to an endtime revival and historical movements in the church such as the Jesus Movement. Bishop Dr. Bill Hamon has also given and received prophecies related to historical movements, and has written several books concerning that and recently Rick Joyner published a prophetic dream from a friend in ministry involving a large caliber rifle that killed the great bear of 1929 (reference to the Great Depression) and an inscription on a plaque next to the gun regarding intercession strategy. In the dream, another gun and plaque were prepared for the current economic crisis.

So, in general the concept of Calendar Prophecy involves important dates in history, anniversaries, or some other element of time. This type could just as well be called Commemorative Prophecy, since much of the prophetic focus is on specific dates, months, memorials, anniversaries, etc. We have already discussed the role of memory in prophecy. Some prophecy has specific timelines attached. If you receive a word that says, "In the next three months, such and such will come to pass, or you will see an increase or improvement in your finances in 60 days," then that aspect is a Calendar Prophecy.

11) Counterfeit Prophecy

The next type is **Counterfeit Prophecy.** Counterfeit Prophecy is prophecy from different types of spirits. This would not typically be called real or legitimate prophecy but instead originates from demonic sources and produces demonically-inspired prophecies that come through other spirits than the spirit of God. They can come from a psychic or medium or a sorcerer or warlock or witch or coven or black magic or dark power source. They can come from a new age spirit where there is channeling and levitation and all these counterfeit signs like spells, séances, divinations or incantations. And they can sometimes come from cults ruled by man. Just look at the disastrous results and loss of life associated with the followers of Jim Jones, David Koresh, and Charles Manson, for example.

All these types of things are called Counterfeit prophecies because they come from counterfeit spirits and not from the spirit of God. They may look like a prophecy. They may have some elements of accuracy or a white lie or there might be one kernel of truth in something that looks plausible or that seems to add some level of credibility. But, the discerning person will understand and know and see what spirit is involved there and will see the lack of fruit in the person's life and understand that it is a Counterfeit Prophecy.

Certainly the spirit of Samuel accurately foretold King Saul's death after the witch of Endor conjured up his spirit at Saul's request. But, that is a sin called necromancy, which was punishable by death in the Old Testament. It was a sad indictment that the king of Israel had more confidence in a dead prophet than in the living prophets of God. So, Saul paid with his life the following day, and three of his sons, including the heir apparent, Jonathan, died with him in battle as God effected a generational leadership transfer. (1 Sam. 28:16-20, 31:1-3) Isa. 8:19 says, *"When men tell you to consult mediums and spiritists, who whisper and mutter, should not a people inquire of their God? Why consult the dead on behalf of the living?"* (NIV)

According to research cited by Rick Joyner, Christians in the U.S. spent $12 billion a year on psychic hotlines in a recent year. This is an indictment, not of prophecy, but of the unbelief of many Christians and Christian leaders who would rather have their palms read or consult a horoscope or a psychic or a medium than learn how to hear God's voice for themselves or consult a true prophet of God.

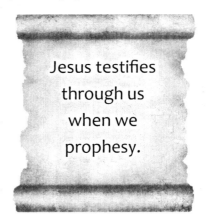

Jesus testifies through us when we prophesy.

Colossians 2:8 states, *"Watch out for people who try to dazzle you with big words and intellectual double-talk. They want to drag you off into endless arguments that never amount to anything. They spread their ideas through the empty traditions of human beings and the empty superstitions of spirit beings. But that's not the way of Christ. Everything of God gets expressed in him, so you can see and hear him clearly.* **You don't need a telescope, a microscope, or a horoscope to realize the fullness of Christ, and the emptiness of the universe without him.** *When you come to him, that fullness comes together for you, too. His power extends over everything"* (MSG, author's emphasis). That verse provides a great summary of why we need the real (Jesus) versus the counterfeit. Rev. 19:10 says, *"The testimony of Jesus is the spirit of prophecy"* (NIV). So, Jesus is testifying through us when we prophesy.

12) Directional Prophecy

Well-intended advice that is frequently given by senior prophets, apostles or pastors to less experienced novice or junior prophets is, "Don't prophesy about dates, mates or weights while you're learning. Wait until you are mature and seasoned before tackling those bigger life issues." Examples of Directional Prophecy are marriage partners, job assignments, what church to join or attend, what city to live in, who to marry, where to work, where to go to school, what nation or people group to serve as a missionary, etc.

One example of Directional Prophecy is when Agabus the Prophet spoke to Paul the Apostle and did a prophetic act by binding Paul's hands with a belt. He warned Paul not to go to Jerusalem or he would be bound and beaten and mistreated by the Jews, but Paul went anyway.

When Jesus told the disciples to cast their net on the right side of the boat, that was a Directional Prophecy as well as a Commercial Prophecy. So, there is occasionally some overlap between these classes or types of prophecy, and they are not intended to be mutually exclusive.

Often Directional Prophecy addresses "yes—no" questions or decisions that people have either on some action or on the timing of that action. We must be very careful only to speak what the Lord says and not go beyond that or add to that. Let me emphasize that prophecy is not counseling, and should not be used as such.

One of the best examples of Directional Prophecy found in the Bible is found in Acts 16:1-10. In verse 6 Paul and his companions were kept by the Holy Spirit from preaching in the province of Asia. In verse 7 the Spirit would not allow them to enter Bithynia, but in verses 9-10, the Spirit directed Paul and his companions to go to Macedonia, which resulted in many converts, including Lydia and her household.

This concludes our study of the Twelve Types of Prophecy. In the next chapter we will explore Prophetic Creativity.

But he who prophesies
speaks edification
and exhortation and
comfort to men.
1 Corinthians 14:3 NKJV

Chapter Thirteen

Prophetic Creativity

Bezalel and Aholiab were used to construct the exquisite designs of the Tabernacle and its furnishings. God did not commission Moses the Prophet and Apostle to Israel to do the work; instead, He anointed Bezalel and Aholiab, filling them with the Holy Spirit to function in the fullness of wisdom, understanding, knowledge and all manner of workmanship. Working in the strength of that anointing, they were able to deliver what God had shown to Moses on the Mountain (Exodus 31:1-11, 35:30-35, 36:1-7, 37:1-29). Today, prophecy is available to every profession, occupation, craft, trade, sector, and industry, and with Prophetic Creativity, there is such a wide range of expression that is possible.

Similarly, Asaph was gifted for worship and music, and Miriam wrote songs and danced unto the Lord. There is prophetic art, prophetic dance, prophetic sculpture, prophetic painting, prophetic fashion design, prophetic storytelling, prophetic murals, banners and flags, prophetic film, prophetic theatre, prophetic inventions and ideas, prophetic branding and prophetic trade marks, prophetic graphic design, music and worship and prophetic website and prophetic song and the song of the Lord; this is just a small list that I could keep developing. There is prophetic architecture and all of the designs in addition to the prophetic Scripture and the prophetic gift can manifest in any dimension of human enterprise and creative expression; a lot of times people want to just limit prophecy to some personal word that they get. But, it is much deeper, much wider, and much stronger than that, so God's heart is to prophesy to every part of creation and every sector of society, and sphere of influence and that is where creativity comes in.

Creativity is being sensitive to the spirit of God and going beyond our natural capabilities. It is going beyond our natural talents in partnering with the prophetic and partnering with God in whatever it is we are doing at the time. I co-hosted child prodigy Akiane one summer as part of a Visions 777 webinar series with Dr. Joseph Peck.

> Creativity is being sensitive to the spirit of God and going beyond our natural capabilities.

She began drawing at age four, and painting at age five. She had a series of third heaven experiences with Jesus and angels, and used similar language as that included in the earlier chapter on Celestial Prophecy about being "taken up" or "caught up" by the Spirit.

We should be asking God, "What is Your design for this building? What is the bridge for this song that I am writing? What words do you want me to communicate to my audience? God, what is the best ending for this scene or the best ending for this chapter of my book?"

It is tapping into the revelatory realm of God in whatever you are doing. That is how I would define Prophetic Creativity.

However, we can't adequately or fully discuss Prophetic Creativity without making reference to the prophet Ezekiel and his powerful prophetic descriptions of the winged creatures and wheels of fire in Ezekiel Chapter One. His ability to describe minute and profound details is carried on throughout the book when he gave the design and configurations of God's temple in chapters 40 and 41. These descriptions allow the reader to actually visualize the temple of his day and other aspects of Jewish culture with a type of "virtual reality" perspective. No other prophet of the Old Testament painted such a vivid picture for readers as he did.

God's desire to reveal details can be summed up in these verses found in Ezekiel 43:10-12 (KJV):

> *Thou son of man, shew the house to the house of Israel, that they may be ashamed of their iniquities [bad patterns] and let them measure the pattern. And if they be ashamed of all that they have done, shew them the form of the house, and the fashion thereof, and the goings out thereof, and the comings in thereof, and all the forms thereof, and all the ordinances thereof, and all the forms thereof, and all the laws thereof: and write it in their sight, that they may keep the whole form thereof, and all the ordinances thereof, and do them. This is the law of the house; Upon the top of the mountain the whole limit thereof round about shall be most holy. Behold, this is the law of the house."*

God knew that if his people had a thorough description of how he wanted things to be, they would be less prone to develop their own flawed designs. God provides a "baseline" pattern for us to build from. We obviously need this baseline in order to point out flaws in our own design and to build accurately and correctly as we move further into the completion of projects. When we apply "The Law of the House" in prophetic designs, we stay within the allowable limits of godly creativity and will be able to use our own creativity with godly influences as we build.

A final example of Prophetic Creativity is prophetic acts. Some examples from the Old Testament include the prophet telling the king to strike the arrows on the ground, Naaman dipping seven times in the Jordan River to be cleansed of his leprosy, and various leaders rending their garments as a sign of repentance. Hosea was told to marry a prostitute (named Gomer) and then redeem her after she left him. Isaiah was told by God to walk around naked and barefoot for three years in precession of the King of Assyria being led away stripped and barefoot to Egypt's shame. One of the most extreme prophetic acts that spanned more than a year is recorded in Ezekiel 4-5. In the New Testament, Jesus spit in the dirt making mud, applying it to the eyes of a blind man, then healed him. In Acts, Agabus bound the hands of Paul with a belt telling him, *"Such will happen to the man who wears this belt and goes to Jerusalem."* Such prophetic acts are also common in land repentance ceremonies such as pouring oil on the ground, breaking sticks, burying Bibles, pouring salt in bodies of water and other symbolic activities.

This concludes our review of Prophetic Creativity. In the next chapter we will cover Prophetic Perversion.

Chapter Fourteen

Prophetic Perversion

We cannot, no, we must not, use our prophetic gift, mantle, unction or office to become prophetic mercenaries (hired guns), prophetic perjurers (those who give false testimony against others and against God), prophetic pickpockets, prophetic prostitutes, or prophetic profilers (targeting wealthy people, especially businessmen or middle-aged and elderly single women, for greedy selfish gain), as some in the prophetic community have done and are doing. Such acts of perversion are repeatedly condemned in Scripture (see 1 Tim. 1:8-11, for example).

Some of these so-called prophets act more like drug dealers or pimps or concert promoters with their $50 lines, $100 lines, $500 lines, $1,000 lines, and $5,000 lines, etc. or their Bronze, Silver, Gold, Diamond and Platinum Prophetic Packages. In my opinion, such people are carnal and deceived and are ministering after the flesh and not after the Spirit; they are deceived and already under judgment whether they know it or not, and even worse, they tarnish the mission, purpose and reputation of the prophetic and true prophets by so doing these things. It's time that the prophetic community begin policing itself and publishing standards of ministry, conduct and ethics. Have you ever heard of a $5 healing or a $50 healing or a $500 healing or a $5000 healing? Have you ever heard of a $5 salvation or a $50 salvation or a $500 salvation or a $5000 salvation? Of course not. Such concepts and terms would be an abomination and a reproach on the church and the people who practiced such things. Well, prophecy is no different in that regard.

All healing and salvation comes from the Spirit of God as a divine gift in response to faith. The prophetic gift and all other charismatic gifts function and operate in this same way. So, let those among us who are seasoned and mature in the prophetic, admonish and teach and correct and try to restore those who are not, in a spirit of love and humility and gentleness. Those who are unwilling to repent of such practices should be marked in the spirit, as Titus 3:10-11 teaches us, to mark those who walk divisively and disorderly among us, and report them to the church and have nothing further to do with them.

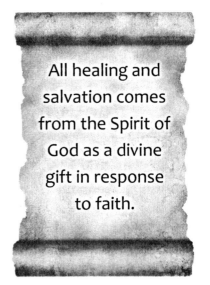

All healing and salvation comes from the Spirit of God as a divine gift in response to faith.

The Bible records a few such examples of lying prophets, and prophets that were for hire. These would include the servant of the prophet Elisha, named Gehazi, who chased after Naaman to get two talents of silver and two changes of clothes when Elisha his master had said he didn't want any gifts and had told Naaman to take his entourage and gifts back home. Gehazi first lied to Naaman.

Then Gehazi compounded his sin by hiding these items in his living quarters and lying to Elisha about where he had been and what he had done. Because of that, he and his entire family received a curse of leprosy from that day on.

Balaam was another example of prophetic perjury who was influenced by Mammon. He was a prophet of God and he was so stubborn, hard-hearted, and blinded by Mammon that his donkey had to prophesy to him. God put an angel in the path of the donkey as he was riding to go to the foreign king in opposition and disobedience to what God had told him. If the donkey had not swerved out of the way, then the angel of God was about to kill this errant prophet.

Then Balaam went to different high places with this foreign king and the king gave him money and other rewards and tried to get him to prophesy against Israel, but every time he prophesied, it was for Israel because the Spirit would not allow him to prophesy otherwise. But, after that, he gave the king a demonic strategy because of the spirit of sorcery and divination that was operating in him of how to seduce Israel and cause them to sin by sending foreign women into the Israelite camp. The strategy worked.

Because of that, the Lord's anger burned against them and He sent a plague over Israel that killed 24,000 people in the camp because of their disobedience, before Moses intervened and asked God for mercy. Ultimately, this cost Balaam his life (Numbers 31:8, Joshua 13:22), and he died by the sword. So, Prophetic Perversion deals with and refers to people that abuse and misuse their prophetic gift, mantle, unction or office, and lack mature character.

I have seen prophets who are only interested in prophesying for money, and it is not a pretty sight. They do not care about other people and don't love people. They don't even love God.

Their true love and first love is money, or should I say Mammon? They see their prophetic gift as a way to make money and gain trust and credibility and create a platform from which to coerce and manipulate people. I call them prophetic pickpockets and prophetic prostitutes and wolves in sheep's clothing because they simply try to gain people's trust, confidence, loyalty and allegiance through their prophetic gift and through flattery and deception for their own self-gain and self-promotion at the expense of others. Obviously those are wrong motives for ministry and that is really important and a big deal to God. He cares deeply for His children. Those who abuse His children in this way will come under His judgment.

God is much less concerned about someone's prophetic gift, mantle, unction or office than He is with the motives of their heart and their character. I'd much rather minister prophetically with a six-year-old child who has never prophesied a day in his or her life than minister with someone with wrong motives or a wrong heart, because God is not going to bless that.

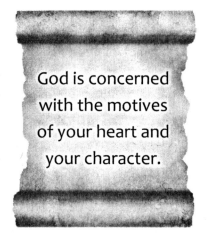

God is concerned with the motives of your heart and your character.

So, I admonish you who are reading this to minister "as unto the Lord," and to be profitable stewards of the grace and gift bestowed upon you by the Lord. Realize that you are His ambassador to a lost, dying and hurting world. Leave the world a better place than you found it and occupy until He comes.

This concludes our review of Prophetic Perversion and now we will explore Prophetic Promises in the next chapter.

Chapter Fifteen

Prophetic Promises

Have you ever had a promise from God? If so, you are in good company, and in good hands. God is a promise-keeping God, and the Bible is full of promises. This is part of the covenantal blessing from our covenant-keeping God. Different writers give different estimates of the total number of such promises, ranging from 3,000 to 10,000. A familiar promise that many Christians quote is Rom. 8:28, "*For all things work together for good for those who are in Christ Jesus, and are called according to His purpose.*" (NIV) Another promise that we stand on is Psalm 91:1, "*He who dwells in the secret place of the Most High Shall abide under the shadow of the Almighty.*" (KJV) One of my favorites is Luke 1:37, "*For with God nothing shall be impossible.*" Another is John 12:24, (NIV) "*Very truly I tell you, unless a kernel of wheat falls to the ground and dies, it remains only a single seed. But if it dies, it produces many seeds.*"

I have also had several personal, Prophetic Promises from God. They either have come to pass, or they will come to pass. God's word is yes and amen through Christ Jesus (2 Cor. 1:20). The NIV translation says, *"For no matter how many promises God has made, they are "Yes" in Christ. And so through him the "Amen" is spoken by us to the glory of God."* The Amplified version puts it this way: *"For as many as are the promises of God, they all find their Yes [answer] in Him [Christ]. For this reason we also utter the Amen (so be it) to God through Him [in His Person and by His agency] to the glory of God."*

If we were using baseball terminology, we would say God is batting .1000. God has an excellent track record of keeping His word, and a long list of those who can testify and witness to that. A few examples would include Noah, Abraham, Sarah, Isaac, Jacob, Joseph, Moses, Joshua, Deborah, Barak, Gideon, David, Daniel, Cyrus, Mary the mother of Jesus, John the Baptist, Jesus, Peter, Paul, John, etc. Numbers 23:19 (KJV) says, *"God is not a man, that he should lie; neither the son of man, that he should repent: hath he said, and shall he not do it? or hath he spoken, and shall he not make it good?"*

Regarding Abraham, the Bible says, *"When God made his promise to Abraham, he backed it to the hilt, putting his own reputation on the line. He said, 'I promise that I'll bless you with everything I have— bless and bless and bless!' Abraham stuck it out and got everything that had been promised to him. When people make promises, they guarantee them by appeal to some authority above them so that if there is any question that they'll make good on the promise, the authority will back them up. When God wanted to guarantee his promises, he gave his word, a rock-solid guarantee—God can't break his word. And because his word cannot change, the promise is likewise unchangeable. We who have run for our very lives to God have every reason to grab the promised hope with both hands and never let go.*

It's an unbreakable spiritual lifeline, reaching past all appearances right to the very presence of God where Jesus, running on ahead of us, has taken up his permanent post as high priest for us, in the order of Melchizedek."(AMP)

I recently finished writing and editing a five-volume apostolic anthology in the last year which is titled *Aligning with the Apostolic: An Anthology of Apostleship, Vols. 1-5*. Seventy other apostles and apostolic leaders participated as Contributing Authors by writing and submitting a chapter or chapters on a topic of their choice. I am amazed at how the anthology flows together seamlessly as one voice. This was not even on my radar screen when Mark Gurley prophesied April 9, 2011 that I would write a companion work and sequel to *Partnering with the Prophetic* about the apostolic. Fifteen months later (July 9, 2012) I started on it, and it was finished and sent to press some nine to ten months later in the spring of 2013.

Another such Prophetic Promise involves the nation of Canada. In October 2010 Apostle Curtis Gillespie, Director of the SCOPE Vision group, prophesied over me that God would open a door and give me favor and a platform in Canada to prophesy to the nation, and to help positively impact the economy there. At that time I had never ministered in Canada before and had no plans to go there, although I had been a tourist on several occasions and had grown to admire and appreciate the people, culture, work ethic, ingenuity, hospitality, fortitude, natural resources and rugged beauty of Canada and its citizens.

Several months later, in the spring of 2011, I received a phone call from a pastor and entrepreneur in Grande Prairie, Alberta, Canada named Charlie Fisher, who had discovered one of my web sites and was calling to get acquainted and connect. After a number of phone calls and emails over the next several months, we made plans to meet during the weekend of July 9th-11th in Gig Harbor, Wash. Our meeting quickly grew to include 50 leaders and made an impact on and left a deposit in the region, and produced lasting fruit. The next month (Aug.) Charlie invited me to come to Grande Prairie and speak on 11-11-11 at an event he felt led to organize. The following month (Sept.) he asked me to invite some of our K.E.Y.S. network leaders as well, and to quickly organize a KEYS Canada event for the weekend of 11-11-11.

An amazing outpouring of the Spirit occurred on 11-11-11 and great fruit resulted, including a shift in the spiritual and financial atmosphere over the city. That led to a follow-up meeting on 12-12-12 in Grande Prairie called U.N.K.A.P., which involved some of the same people, built on the earlier success and produced similar results, shifts and breakthroughs in the city and region. Prophet Charlie Robinson said that something was released for the nation at this event on 12-12-12, and Dennis Wiedrick confirmed that, and had a dramatic 3rd heaven vision which he released publicly during the last session of the conference. Many attendees were also healed of sickness and disease. Several leaders who attended this event have subsequently been commissioned and ordained in five-fold ministry.

In between these two events, I was invited by Mike and Sharon Molnar to speak at their ICCC Canada event in Niagara Falls, Ontario, Canada in late April, 2012. Mike and Sharon had attended our KEYS LA event the month before in Southern California and we had gotten acquainted and become friends. The Holy Spirit showed up in power at both events, and made an impact on both Los Angeles and Niagara Falls, and the leaders who attended these events. The prophetic word I had received about Canada quickly came to pass!

Another Prophetic Promise involves the house my wife and I are living in now in Lakebay, Wash. We moved here April 15, 2013 after the Holy Spirit made it clear during Christmas 2012 and January 2013 that our time in Texas was up, and that the new season we were entering required a new location and new relationships and alignment. The Lord said He wanted to expand our territory, and indeed He did.

On Oct. 1, 2011 my wife, Caroline, had an open vision in which she saw a large wooden house with a cathedral ceiling in the upper level, and large evergreen trees on the sides and at the back of the property, and a body of water beyond the trees in back. She heard the Lord say, "This house is in Washington State and you will own it in the future," and she also saw an envelope with a letter of invitation, and a sum of money inside, in the vision. She told me about the vision later that day, and I asked her to draw a picture of what she had seen and write down the details, which she did. I then three-hole-punched her paper and added it in Volume Three of our prophetic notebooks for safekeeping, later reference and prayer.

When I returned home to Texas from the 12-12-12 event in western Canada, a few days before Christmas, I told my wife that I felt different in my spirit and that something had shifted inside of me and I no longer felt like I belonged in Austin or Texas after nearly 26 years there. During our Christmas break with family, we received a phone call and an investor couple made an unsolicited offer on the house we had been living in for the last 9.5 years, and after meeting with us shortly after New Year's, the offer was accepted by the owners (friends I had married years before) and the house sold and closed at the end of January. We had opted not to buy the house because it was too small for the vision the Lord had shown us and the style and layout were not to our preference or heart's desire. We signed a short-term lease before the sale to give me time to wrap up some current work-related projects, find another house to purchase or lease or rent, and begin packing for the upcoming move.

When we knew in early January that the house we were living in was going to sell, we met with our local pastors who served as our apostolic spiritual covering, and began praying with them about where and what the Lord had for us in this season. I also notified our intercession teams, and they began praying about this also. One night as I was going to bed, I heard a sound from my cell phone, signifying that a text or email had arrived. When I checked the phone, which was on my night stand, I noticed a new email from a real estate broker friend from Washington State. The Holy Spirit spoke to me and told me to read the email first thing the next morning, which I did. To my surprise, the email contained a listing for a house in Washington that had a monthly payment the same as our house in Texas. I told the broker to send me more listings in that price range, and two emails later, I saw the house listed that we now own and live in in Washington. To test the water, so to speak, I called a mortgage banker in Washington who was referred to us, and we were pre-approved for a mortgage loan in a ten-minute phone call. More confirmation.

As it became increasingly clear to us that the Lord wanted us to move to the Seattle area, and was giving us the desire of our hearts concerning a house and acreage, I remembered the vision my wife had had 18 months ago, and looked up the paper with the drawing and the details of the house she had seen. To my utter amazement and astonishment, it matched exactly the house we were about to make an offer on. As if to put an exclamation point on this, the day we had planned to make an offer, the bank which was selling the house lowered the price by $10,500, to the very price we had planned to offer. We made a written offer the next day, it was accepted, and the rest is history, as they say. Since moving here, we have felt the tangible peace and presence of the Holy Spirit, and have observed angels on the property. Many guests have sensed a portal here and have mentioned experiencing an open heaven atmosphere.

The rest of my wife's vision is also coming to pass, as we received a letter of invitation from several five-fold leaders in the county we moved to prior to making an offer on the house, and the sum of money she saw is also in process and has been identified. To go along with her vision, I received a prophecy in Dec. 2011 from a trusted apostle who I am in covenant with that the Lord would deploy me to the Seattle region and the State of Washington in the future. This apostle saw a vision of me in the foreground and Mount Rainier in the background—a scene I have witnessed numerous times since moving here.

Lest you think we have an inside track or special advantage in seeing our Prophetic Promises fulfilled, there are numerous other prophecies that one or both of us have received which have not yet come to pass. We wait patiently and pray earnestly and believe fully and contend forcefully for these to manifest, in God's timing and in God's way. I encourage you to do the same. In closing this chapter, a final Scripture comes to mind. 2 Peter 1:3-4 (NIV) says, *"His divine power has given us everything we need for a godly life through our knowledge of him who called us by his own glory and goodness. Through these he has given us **his very great and precious promises**, so that through them you may participate in the divine nature, having escaped the corruption in the world caused by evil desires"* (author's emphasis).

The Lord's promises are keys to the divine nature, and Prophetic Promises are keys to unlock or unfold our destiny. As we draw to a close here with this discussion, in the next chapter, we will explore Prophetic Partnerships.

Then the word of
the Lord came to
me, saying: "Before
I formed you in the
womb I knew you;
Before you were born
I sanctified you; I
ordained you a prophet
to the nations."
Jeremiah 1:4-5 NKJV

Chapter Sixteen

Prophetic Partnership

Everyone partners with something so the only question is, "What will you partner with?" If God's people do not partner with the prophetic, they will partner with other things. Often God's people in the Old Testament partnered with the idols and false gods of the people living around them. On one occasion they made a golden calf and began to worship it. God became so angry that He wanted to destroy them, but Moses intervened and God withdrew His judgment after He sent a plague and 3,000 men died by the sword at the hands of the Levites. God told His people they would prosper if they obeyed His prophets, but many chose disobedience and rebellion and stubbornness instead.

It is much the same today, although the life and death and resurrection of Jesus have ushered in the New Testament and the Kingdom of God. Modern-day believers also have direct access to the written word of God through the Scriptures and the voice of God through the Holy Spirit living inside of us. God did not stop speaking after He created the universe, our galaxy and planet Earth, all living creatures, and mankind. He continued to speak to Adam and Eve, to the judges and prophets, to Abraham, Isaac, Jacob and Joseph, to Jesus and his disciples, and He continues to speak to you and me today. The question remains: "What will you partner with?" The prophetic must also partner with the other five-fold ministries, and in particular, must work closely with the apostolic.

Prophetic Partnership is the next-to-last chapter in the book and builds upon everything else that we have covered. Essentially, everyone is going to partner with something, whether you are Christian or whether you are a non-Christian. You are going to be partnering with things. You will be partnering with ideas, with what you believe is true. You will be partnering with values. You will be partnering with culture. You will be partnering with people. And, you will be partnering with a kingdom. So, the question and the challenge for you is: With whom or what will you be partnering?

God wants the church to partner with His Spirit, and the gifts of the Spirit. He has been really clear on that in His Word, as we have discussed, and one of the things that the church needs to partner with is the prophetic. People should not partner with idols, with false gods and the spiritually uncircumcised people around them. For doing that in the Old Testament the Israelites came under God's judgment. They made a golden calf on one occasion

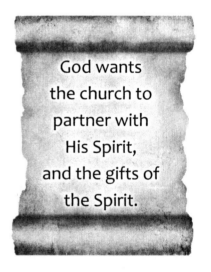

God wants the church to partner with His Spirit, and the gifts of the Spirit.

and God judged and punished them for that. It is much the same today. Modern-day believers have access to the written Word of

God through the Scriptures. We also have access to the voice of God through the Holy Spirit on the inside of us.

God did not stop speaking after He created the universe. After He had planned the earth and all the living creatures and mankind, he continued to speak to Adam and Eve. He spoke to the prophets, to the judges and to the kings. He spoke to Abraham, Isaac and Jacob and to Joseph. He spoke to Jesus. He spoke to the twelve Apostles, and many of the disciples like Philip, who had four prophetic daughters. He spoke to Simeon, Anna, and John the Baptist. He continues to speak to you and me today and to all who will listen and obey His voice and commands.

First of all, on the individual level, we as Christians have to decide to partner with the prophetic. Then on the corporate level, God wants the leadership of the church to partner with the prophetic and also the prophetic has to partner with the other five-fold gifts and ministries. The prophetic has to partner with the gift of teaching. The prophetic has to partner with the gift of pastoring. The prophetic has to partner with evangelism and there are several excellent books written about prophetic evangelism. The prophetic has to partner with the apostolic. In fact, the apostolic and the prophetic are so closely aligned that it is more like a marriage than a partnership because they really have to depend heavily on each other. So, this is what I am talking about when I mention or refer to Prophetic Partnership. God has designed the prophetic to be a blessing, to be part of the foundation of the church, but also to be something that His people partner with.

A good example of Prophetic Partnership is found in Ezra 5:16 where a construction project had begun without success in getting it finished. *"Then came the same Sheshbazzar, and laid the* *foundation of the house of God which is at Jerusalem: and since that time even until now hath it been in building, **and yet is not finished.***"

There needed to be the addition of prophetic technology in order to take the project to the stage of completion that it needed.

Ezra 6:14-15 says, *"And the elders of the Jews builded, **and they prospered through the prophesying** of Haggai the prophet and Zecharaiah the son of Iddo. And they builded, **and finished it,** according to the commandment of the God of Israel, and according to the commandment of Cyrus, and Darius, and Artaxerxes king of Persia. And this house was finished on the third day of the month of Adar, which was in the sixth year of the reign of Darius the king."* (KJV, author's emphasis)

There was a major project at hand and the collective efforts of everyone involved were enhanced by prophecy. The work prospered through prophesying. The term *prospered* is from the Hebrew word *Tsaleach,* meaning: To push forward, break out, be profitable, or to have effect (Strong's). The addition or injection of strong prophetic words will often cut down on production time or facilitate a better use of resources during a major project. Without a doubt, prophetic words and visions are one of the most powerful architectural technologies available today for completing the work of God in the marketplace and the municipality (government).

> Prophetic words and visions are powerful to complete the work of God in the marketplace and the municipality.

There is a Scripture saying that if you receive a prophet in the name of a prophet that you will receive a prophet's reward. Another Scripture says God does nothing except He tells His servants the prophets of His plans and secrets. God has clearly not stopped talking to people. He has not stopped talking to prophets. He has not stopped distributing prophetic gifts and mantles to His body as He sees fit. So, it is time for us to partner with the prophetic, and for the prophetic to partner with the other five-fold functions. Only then can the Kingdom of God be established in the earth, can we occupy until He comes, and can the church become the governmental agent of transformation that it was created to be.

As we close here, I invite you to pray this prayer of activation:

Father in heaven, please activate, release, and/or impart every natural and spiritual gift that you have designed, intended and purposed for me from before the foundations of the world. Anything in me that is asleep, dormant, buried, on the shelf, stuck, stagnant, dead, unopened, unwrapped, unclaimed or unwanted—I invite You to wake up, shake up, shape up, uncover, resurrect, mobilize, dislodge, prune, open, unwrap, activate, energize, and engage every natural and spiritual gift inside of me. Please remove any veils or scales from my eyes and my heart. I renounce and break agreement with any lie from the evil one and invite Your truth to fill and flood my heart, soul, mind and spirit. I repent for any way(s) that I have been displeasing or disobedient to You and I agree with heaven. I receive everything You have in store for me now as a wise steward and faithful and beloved son or daughter of the Most High God. I decree and declare this done now in Jesus' name. Amen.

But Jesus said to them, "A prophet is not without honor except in his own country, among his own relatives, and in his own house."

Mark 6:4-5 NKJV

Judging Prophecy

J udging prophecy is in danger of becoming a lost art in the church and in the modern world. It requires grace, love, maturity and wisdom, and for the most part, it is a thankless and unglamorous job. Many churches as well as other organizations have no grid or mechanism or context or culture for receiving or judging prophecies. Even in churches or organizations that do, most prophets have sometimes had their words judged improperly, or not at all, or have been rubber stamped or misunderstood or abused in the judging process. There are many reasons for this, which we will try and touch on briefly here. Judging prophecy is both an expression and administration of spiritual fatherhood or motherhood, and the proper exercise thereof teaches one to make distinctions between the necessary and the optional, the ready and the not ready, the appropriate and the inappropriate, the exceptional and the mundane.

Prophets have one piece of a larger pie. Judging prophecy helps us to see the bigger picture, and if not the whole pie, at least more of it. The Bible says that we see in part, know in part, and prophesy in part. *"For we know in part and we prophesy in part. But when that which is perfect has come, then that which is in part will be done away. When I was a child, I spoke as a child, I understood as a child, I thought as a child; but when I became a man, I put away childish things. For now we see in a mirror, dimly, but then face to face. Now I know in part, but then I shall know just as I also am known"* (1 Cor. 13:9-12, NKJV, author's emphasis).

It is no accident that the gift of prophecy is mentioned just a few verses earlier in that chapter in the context of love. *"If I have the gift of prophecy and can fathom all mysteries and all knowledge, and if I have a faith that can move mountains, but do not have love, I am nothing"* (1 Cor. 13:2, NIV, author's emphasis). Another translation says, *"And if I have prophetic powers ([a]the gift of interpreting the divine will and purpose), and understand all the secret truths and mysteries and possess all knowledge, and if I have [sufficient] faith so that I can remove mountains, but have not love (God's love in me) I am nothing (a useless nobody)"* (1 Cor. 13:2, AMP, author's emphasis).

So, one of the chief aims in both prophesying and judging prophecy, is to show forth God's love, as well as His wisdom, grace, power and other attributes and qualities of His divine nature. The bottom line is one cannot prophesy or judge prophecy effectively without having God's love. Paul the Apostle said, *"It's more important that everyone have access to the knowledge and love of God in language everyone understands than that you go off and cultivate God's presence in a mysterious prayer language—unless, of course, there is someone who can interpret what you are saying for the benefit of all"* (1 Cor. 14:5, MSG, author's emphasis).

Paul writes elsewhere, "*Don't suppress the Spirit, and **don't stifle those who have a word from the Master. On the other hand, don't be gullible. Check out everything, and keep only what's good. Throw out anything tainted with evil**"* (1 Thess. 5:19-22, MSG, author's emphasis). Another translation of this passage says, "*Do not quench (suppress or subdue) the [Holy] Spirit; **Do not spurn the gifts and utterances of the prophets [do not depreciate prophetic revelations nor despise inspired instruction or exhortation or warning]. But test and prove all things** [until you can recognize] what is good; [to that] hold fast*" (1 Thess. 5:19-21, AMP, author's emphasis). So, the definition of judging prophecy in this passage, is to check out everything, test and prove all things, keep only what's good, and throw out (reject or discard) anything tainted with evil (impure, polluted, or poisonous).

It is important to note that all Christians are admonished and exhorted to prophesy and to eagerly and earnestly desire to prophesy (1 Cor. 14:5, 39; Joel 2:28). Even Moses told Joshua, "*I wish that all the Lord's people were prophets and that the Lord would put his Spirit on them*" (Num. 11:29, NIV). In fact, some of the most significant prophecies in history and in church revivals have come from those who are young and inexperienced in the Lord and in spiritual gifts. The proverbial saying "*Out of the mouth of babes*" has its roots and origins in Scripture (Ps. 8:2, Matt. 21:16) as a prophecy. Therefore, it is important to create an atmosphere and environment conducive to prophecy that

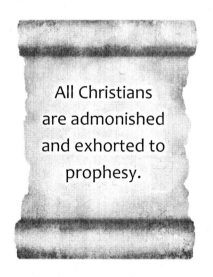

All Christians are admonished and exhorted to prophesy.

is a safe place for the whole spectrum of prophetic expression, maturity and community.

A related Scripture says, *"Let two or three prophets speak, and let the others judge"* (1 Cor. 14:29, NKJV). The Greek word for "prophets" is *prophetes*, meaning: a foreteller, inspired speaker, poet or general meaning of a prophet. The Greek word for "speak" is *laleo*, meaning to talk, utter words, preach, tell or say. The Greek word for "others" is *allos*, meaning: another, same, similar, more than one. The Greek word for "judge" is *diakrino*, meaning: **to separate thoroughly, to make different, to decide, discern, be partial to** (Strong's, emphasis added). *"So let two or three prophets speak [those inspired to preach or teach], while the rest **pay attention and weigh and discern** what is said"* (1 Cor. 14:29, AMP, author's emphasis). *"Two or three prophets should speak, and the others should **evaluate**"* (1 Cor. 14:29, CSB, author's emphasis). Among the most useful meanings of "judge" listed here for our purposes are to **pay attention** (listen intently and possibly even take notes or listen to the audio recording later), **weigh, evaluate, decide, discern, to separate thoroughly**, and **be partial to** (we are to be partial to the truth).

This verse of Scripture is made clearer when examined in context. *"So let two or three prophets speak [those inspired to preach or teach], while the rest pay attention and weigh and discern what is said. But if an inspired revelation comes to another who is sitting by, then let the first one be silent. **For in this way you can give testimony [prophesying and thus interpreting the divine will and purpose] one by one, so that all may be instructed and all may be stimulated and encouraged;** For the spirits of the prophets (the speakers in tongues) are under the speaker's control [and subject to being silenced as may be necessary], **For He [Who is the source of their prophesying] is not a God of confusion and disorder but of peace and order. As [is the practice] in all the churches of the saints (God's people),"* (1 Cor. 14: 29-33, AMP, author's emphasis). So, the context here is maintaining order and peace in a corporate assembly while expressing spiritual gifts, and these are procedural and logistical instructions and directives for how to do that in a group setting — generally, a church service, and more specifically, prophecy.

Part of the dysfunction that has arisen around this whole process is that prophetic judgment typically only occurs when there is a perceived issue or problem with a prophecy. So, for many of God's prophets, all they have ever experienced is negative reinforcement. Some prophets have gone through life with never having had a single prophecy judged, or at least never having received verbal or written feedback of the prophetic judgment. Part of the reason why is expediency (if it's not broke, why fix it?), and another part is time constraints. Many church services, conferences and board meetings have tight schedules and fairly rigid time constraints, and taking time to judge prophecy publicly is not a part of the normal schedule or program, and usually only occurs when something is seriously wrong with the prophecy given, and damage control is needed, or doctrinal correction is required, or a core protocol has been breached.

Fortunately, these type of things happen only infrequently or rarely, and true prophecy always works the other way and produces and/or releases encouragement, hope, edification, comfort, equipping, strengthening, understanding, impartation, activation, peace, joy and other positive benefits in the hearers. In fact, a "word in season" and a "fitly framed word" can have a catalytic effect and break open a meeting by releasing the Spirit of God in a fresh, original, authentic way. Additionally, prophecy is often confirming to those receiving it and whoever is speaking and bringing the main message in a service or meeting.

Moreover, it is almost always best to judge prophecies in private after a service is over or a few days later so that the people involved are not rushed and have time to reflect upon the word and listen to it several times if necessary, pray into it for additional discernment, understanding, interpretation and/or application, and can give adequate evaluation and feedback to the person who prophesied. This is best done in person so that body language, facial expression, eye contact and other secondary data are available to the parties involved, but can be done over the phone or via Skype® or Go to Meeting® if necessary, so that two-way communication can still occur, albeit on a more limited basis. Only under extreme circumstances should judging prophecy be handled via email or a letter, as a last resort.

The same is true of board meetings or other group functions in the marketplace. Afterwards, the prophecies given at events many times do not seem as important, or urgent, and are often overlooked, neglected or forgotten in our rush to get to the next item on the agenda, or on our list of things to do. Another reason prophecy is not always judged in real time is that no one present may have a complete or accurate interpretation at the moment of what the prophecy means, or how to apply it, especially if it includes visions. So, unless public correction is needed, either immediately or as soon as possible, it is best to judge prophecy in private after the fact, for the reasons stated above.

Related to the verses cited in 1 Cor., numerous Scriptures say both God and man will establish a thing at the mouth of two or three witnesses (Deut. 17:6, 19:15; Matt. 18:16; 2 Cor. 13:1; 1 Tim. 5:19; Heb. 10:28). The witnesses are a vital part of the judging process. The credibility of witnesses is an important factor in legal and court proceedings and outcomes, and there are different categories of witnesses, including those who are part of the witness protection program, eyewitnesses, and expert witnesses, to name a few. Those who judge prophecy should be those considered by other leaders to be expert in things of the spirit in general, and prophecy and revelation in particular. They should be those who are proven, tested, trusted, seasoned, wise and discerning in spiritual matters and spiritual gifts, including prophecy.

As a general guideline, those authorized to judge prophecy, according to Scripture, are apostles, prophets, and elders. Now elders, as the biblical model of government for local churches, may delegate judging prophecy to other five-fold leaders in their churches, rather than do it themselves. Typically, though, there will be apostles or prophets represented among the eldership of churches adhering to and following the biblical pattern and model of church government. However, that is not always the case in many modern churches, especially considering that 80% of all churches have less than 200 members (Karl Vaters, http://newsmallchurch. com/why-80-percent-will-never-break-the-200-barrier/).

In any event, the word *allos* is definitive and controlling in this regard, and means **additional ones of the same kind or type** (see Matt. 2:12, 4:21, 13:24; John 14:16), while *heteros* means additional ones of a different kind or type (see Gal. 1:6-7; Rom. 7:23; Matt. 11:3; Luke 23:32; Acts 7:18, 27:1). *Allos* expresses a numerical difference and *heteros* expresses a qualitative difference. These two words are not interchangeable (see 1 Cor. 15:39-41, Vine's).

I believe it is dangerous to base or build an entire process of judging on one word from Scripture (*allos*) since the definitions from Strong's and Vine's can be interpreted in different ways. I.e., the word *allos* could mean other prophets, other revelators (prophets, apostle-prophets and prophetic apostles), or others in authority with prophetic gifting (prophetic elders and prophetic pastors). I personally believe it means or at least applies to all three, using the principles of hermeneutics to harmonize other Scriptures with these and to see and understand that the context and emphasis of Paul the Apostle's comments in both 1 Cor. and 1 Thess. is order rather than judging.

Apostles and prophets are different than other church or spiritual leaders and five-fold ministers and/or officers in at least three respects. First, they are listed first and second, respectively, in terms of time, place, order and function in Eph. 4:11 and 1 Cor. 12:28. Second, they are the only two officers listed as being part of the foundation of the church (Eph. 2:20). The Greek word for foundation is *themelios*, meaning: "something that is put down, the substructure of a building" (Strong's). And third, their spiritual gift mix is uniquely revelatory in nature. According to Alan Hirsch and Tim Catchim, in their book *The Permanent Revolution*, what apostles and prophets share in common that makes them distinct from the other five-fold gifts is that they are **generative** in their gifting and function, i.e., able to generate, access, process and/or steward divine revelation for the benefit of others (San Francisco, CA: Jossey-Bass, 2012).

Therefore, it makes sense that the very officers of the church most charged and gifted with revelation and serving as the foundation for others to build upon, would be the ones most qualified to judge prophecy. Additionally, elders historically have been appointed by apostles, or more recently in some Protestant denominations, elected, to govern over the affairs of the local church and to set and enforce policy (Acts 14:23, 15:1-35, 16:4; Titus 1:5-9; 1 Tim. 3:1-7). 1 Tim. 4:14 says, *"Do not neglect the gift that is in you, which was given to you by prophecy with the laying on of the hands of the eldership"* (NKJV).

However, not all elders, and not all apostles, are prophetic, or functioning in the gift of prophecy or office of prophet. Those who are should be recognized and sought out when judging prophecy is in order. Furthermore, the common practice in many churches today of not recognizing or acknowledging prophets and prophecy, or even of condemning or dismissing them as irrelevant or nonexistent or fraudulent or heretical, or of only pastors judging prophecy, is unfortunate at best – despite the existence of some heroic, prophetic pastors – and at worst, harmful and damaging to the sheep, keeping them anemic, quenching the Spirit, and only feeding them the logos word and not the rhema word. Prophecy is part of the "whole counsel of God" mentioned in Acts 20:27.

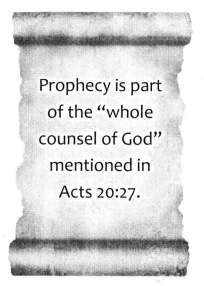

Prophecy is part of the "whole counsel of God" mentioned in Acts 20:27.

Moreover, even among charismatic ministries, churches and leaders, including those of national or international stature and notoriety, there are sharp, frequent and notable disagreements concerning prophecy, beginning with end-time eschatology, and extending to political elections and candidates, to the causes and origins and meanings of natural disasters, and the causes and origins and outcomes of economic cycles and disruptions. These "prophecy predictions," "dueling prophecies," "prophecy philosophies" and divided, split camps and streams within the global charismatic movement, are an indication of and indictment on the lack of prophetic and apostolic fathers and mothers in the church who are true statesmen, the church's antipathy and rejection or ignorance of them for the most part, and the lack of a universally-accepted and agreed-upon process or standard or protocol of judging prophecy. Prophets should not use their reputation or fame or popularity as a bully pulpit or platform to promote their own personal agenda or philosophy at the expense of God's. When they do, they should be held accountable.

The reality is that some of these prophetic leaders who disagree and prophesy opposite futures and outcomes, may at times both be right, in the sense that they are both seeing and hearing things in the Spirit, but one may be a warning of impending judgment or disaster or calamity, and one may be a modern day renaissance or revival or reformation. That is why it is unwise to align with prophetic streams at the expense of the Spirit of God (i.e., "I am of Paul, I am of Apollos," 1 Cor. 3:4-5), but it is wise to align with seasoned, mature prophetic and apostolic fathers and mothers who model and point to Jesus, wherever you can find them.

We will now attempt to remedy this omission of a universally-accepted or standard protocol, by proposing a judging process and set of steps, for others to improve or refine and build upon. First, however, we need to ask a few basic questions. What is the purpose of judging prophecy? And, why did God feel it necessary to safeguard prophecy with the technology of prophetic judgment? I would suggest that the purposes of judging prophecy are: 1) safety and purity for the word of God; 2) safety for the person or persons receiving the prophecy, and for any bystanders, onlookers, crowd or audience present or listening by radio or viewing by television or Internet or wifi-enabled device, podcast, CD or DVD; and 3) safety, training, education, enlightenment, encouragement, edification, accountability, humility and stewardship for the person giving the Word.

Accordingly, we introduce the concept of "prophetic screening" here, as a potential pre-step or pre-condition under certain circumstances, whereby the person who says he or she has a prophetic word or vision to release, but is unknown by the leadership team of whatever meeting or gathering or assembly is being held or taking place, may be asked by one or more of the team leaders to summarize or share their prophecy privately first, before being invited or authorized to release or speak it publicly. There is a reason your parents as a child told you not to take or accept candy from strangers. How much more then should we be on guard not to take or accept prophecy from strangers, unless and until their prophecy has been tested and their identity and character established. "Know those who labor among you."

Another pre-step or pre-condition is knowing who is included in the "others" authorized to judge prophecy in 1 Cor. 14:29. See the earlier lengthy discussion above regarding apostles, prophets, and elders. Those who judge prophecy need to have an understanding of revelation and a mastery of revelatory gifts, and be seasoned and experienced in things of the spirit, including prophecy. They should be those deemed to be impartial and discerning and wise, and to be fathers or mothers in the spirit, and to have a thorough knowledge of and grounding in the word of God, an excellent reputation, and proven character.

Also, we need to address the question of whether it is necessary to have an existing or prior relationship with a person in order to judge their prophecy. The verses which address this process in 1 Cor. and 1 Thess. are based in a local church context, where there is an existing relationship locally between the parties. Although this may not always be possible on a regional or national level, in practice, how effective or useful is the judgment of prophecy if the prophet giving the prophecy being judged does not respect or honor or at least acknowledge those judging his or her prophecy as peers? Anything less may potentially cause or contribute to less than optimal outcomes, including disappointment, resentment or offense. We are not called to be "prophetic policemen."

Let's use foreign policy for nations and governments as an example. Ambassadors only take input, instruction, direction, correction or judgment from other ambassadors or presidents or prime ministers or senates, not from those of lesser standing, stature, position or rank. This serves as a useful analogy for judging prophecy. Anyone can give a prophecy, but ideally only those of equal or higher rank or authority spiritually should judge a prophecy. This will ensure a critique rather than criticism in the judging process. Local prophecies should be judged locally, regional prophecies regionally, and national prophecies nationally. Prophetic judges and judging have been plentiful locally, for the most part, but noticeably absent at the higher levels, when reputations, egos, friendships and/or livelihoods may be at risk or at stake, not to mention nations, economies, lives and souls hanging in the balance. It's time for the spiritual fathers and mothers to come forth, either individually or as councils. Clearly when a public prophecy is false or a nonprophecy, someone should judge it, but deciding who should do so requires wisdom, love, discernment, grace, humility, gentleness and meekness, as well as protocol, precedent and policy.

It is also important to discuss setting briefly, and to distinguish between public and private prophecy. Where, and in what setting, a prophecy is being given, is very important in the understanding and application of the judging process. I would suggest that not all prophecy needs to be judged, or is intended to be judged, for several reasons. The judging process that Paul the Apostle outlined and prescribed for the New Testament churches in 1 Cor. and 1 Thess., as discussed earlier in this chapter, is designed and intended for **public or corporate prophecy**—i.e., prophecy delivered or released in a church or group setting or other public gathering or meeting, such as a conference or corporate assembly. Private (one-on-one or small group) prophecy would be excluded from this judging process, in perhaps most or all cases.

Obviously, there are many occasions of private prophecy that occur, more frequently for some than others, whether it be sharing a word with a co-worker, a neighbor, someone you carpool or ride the bus with, or the person sitting next to you on an airplane, or one of your golf partners, or hunting buddies, or a student at school, or the doctor who is treating your sick relative, or the attorney who is working on your business deal, the teacher at your university, the taxi cab driver, the hotel desk clerk, the waiter or waitress in the restaurant, your roommate or teammate, etc. You get the picture. Prophecy can happen anytime, anywhere, that

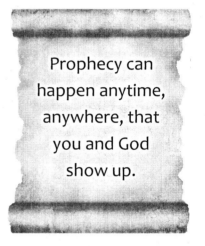

Prophecy can happen anytime, anywhere, that you and God show up.

you and God show up. In many, if not most, such cases, there is no one available or qualified to judge your prophecy except the Holy Spirit. You may not even term what you shared with the person as prophecy if you are operating in stealth mode about how you deliver or describe it.

Additionally, sometimes prophecy is given in the context of a home group, cell group or life group, prophetic training session, school of the prophets, or prophetic workshop, in a less formal setting. So, the process I am proposing here applies to corporate or public (group) prophecy primarily, although the principles can be applied to private (one-on-one or small group) prophecy on an as needed basis.

I have identified nine steps in judging corporate or public (group) prophecy: 1) Judging the words and/or visions prophesied; 2) Judging the spirit of the prophecy; 3) Judging the character of the person giving the prophecy; 4) Judging the delivery of the prophecy; 5) Judging whether the prophecy is aligned and in agreement with Scripture and the nature of God; 6) Judging whether the prophecy is aligned and in agreement with other prophecies from trusted sources; 7) Judging whether the prophecy is aligned and in agreement with history, the laws of science, and other natural laws of the universe; 8) Judging the timing aspect of the prophecy, if any; 9) Judging the interpretation and application of the prophecy, if any. We will now consider and discuss each of these steps in turn.

1. **Judging the words and/or visions prophesied** – Is it from the Lord (yes or no)? Is it for the person prophesying or others or both? Is it for now or the future? Is it a public or private word? Is there an aspect or element of response required? Are they encouraging, edifying, comforting, equipping, exhorting, etc.? Do they make sense and appear to be true *prima facie*? Are they logical or reasonable? Are they uplifting and inspiring? Are they confirming? Do they engage or excite your spirit? Is there life in the prophecy or does it put you to sleep? Does it energize and activate you or bore you? Is the prophecy carrying the DNA and aroma of heaven on it? Does the prophecy accurately represent and portray God's heart on the subjects/topics discussed? Did the prophecy rise above the "noise" level of talk and chatter, and release the sound of heaven in the Spirit realm?

2. **Judging the spirit of the prophecy** – What did the prophecy release in the atmosphere? How did it affect the atmosphere? Did my spirit (the spirit on the inside of me) bear witness with it? Did I have a "check" in my spirit? Did I feel nauseous

or smell a bad odor in the room? Was there a pure flow and clean stream of the Spirit of God coming forth from the prophet, or was there a mixture of spirit and soul/flesh involved or contained in the prophecy? Does the prophecy violate confidentiality, or needlessly hurt others? Does the prophecy draw attention to the prophet, or to God?

3. **Judging the character of the person giving the prophecy** – Are they accountable and in submission to godly authority? Are they known to be living a pure, holy lifestyle? Are they humble and teachable? Are they seeking to please the Lord above self and/or others? Are they transparent? Is there any known, unrepentant sin in their lives? Are they part of an active community of believers or church family? Are they spiritually healthy and growing? Is there fruit in their life and ministry? Do they have a job or income or means of support? Are they part of a healthy family? Are they free from the love of money? Do they have a good reputation? Are they quick to repent if convicted of sin or confronted with error? Do they learn from mistakes and not repeat them? Are they a student of the Word? Do they pray daily?

4. **Judging the delivery of the prophecy** – Was the delivery of the prophecy clear, concise, easy to understand, effective, on the mark, in the zone, well articulated and enunciated? Was the prophecy spoken with authority, boldness and language appropriate for the audience and intended target? Did the prophet draw attention to Jesus in his or her delivery, or to himself/herself? Did the prophet give glory to Jesus or take/keep it for himself/herself? Was the prophecy too long or too short? Was the sound (microphone or voice) too loud or too soft? Did the prophet stay on track and remain laser focused, and avoid

getting into counseling or consulting mode, and stick with prophecy?

5. **Judging whether the prophecy is aligned and in agreement with Scripture and the nature of God** – Does the prophecy contradict or violate or oppose or attempt to refute or challenge Scripture? Does the prophecy line up and support and agree with Scripture? Does the prophecy touch on or draw upon or reference a principle or precedent or example from Scripture? Does the prophecy violate or misrepresent the nature of God?

6. **Judging whether the prophecy is aligned and in agreement with other prophecies from trusted sources** – Are there previous prophecies from this prophet on this subject or to this audience that need to be considered or that have a bearing or effect on what was just prophesied? Are there previous prophecies from other prophets or apostles outside of this setting or metron, or from this local leadership team, that need to be considered or that have a bearing or effect on this word that was just prophesied? Is the prophecy confirming? Is the prophecy part of a larger pattern? Does the prophecy agree with what has been spoken by prophetic intercessors?

7. **Judging whether the prophecy is aligned and in agreement with history, the laws of science, and other natural or spiritual laws or principles** – This test does not always apply, as God can bend or suspend or bypass the laws of nature and science and the universe whenever He chooses to, but it is amazing how many prophecies treat or transgress or trespass on history incorrectly, and include wrong dates and names from history as part of the prophecy. The same

thing applies to science, physics, chemistry, mathematics and other disciplines, canons and fields of inquiry and study. God can and does redeem and reinforce all of these.

8. **Judging the timing of the prophecy, if any** – Was there an element of timing mentioned or implied in the prophecy? Was the prophecy *atemporal* with no time element present? Were there conditions or circumstances of the prophecy that are dependent upon a sequence or chain of events, or a trigger event of some kind to be enacted and manifested? Were there other people mentioned besides the primary recipient whose destinies are either intertwined or may impinge upon or influence the timing of the word's fulfillment or coming to pass? Are there preconditions specified or implied for the prophecy to occur? Did the prophecy suggest or imply or acknowledge a promotion from God or a change in season or transition into a new season?

9. **Judging the interpretation and application of the prophecy, if any** – What response does the Lord require of me, if any, or the person or group receiving the prophecy? What are the key elements of the word or vision? Can they have dual or multiple meanings? Do the symbols or elements in the word or vision have prophetic (spiritual) as well as literal (natural) meaning? What changes or actions, if any, will be required of the recipient(s) for this prophecy to be fulfilled? Was there a suggestion, implication, or requirement for greater character development or training in the person or group or audience receiving the prophecy?

In summary, this brief discussion illustrates the potential complexity of judging prophecy; the various issues to be weighed, evaluated, discerned and/or addressed in the judging process; who should be involved as judges; and the importance of whether the setting is corporate or public (group) or private (one-on-one).

Additionally, there are a few special cases or situations we should mention briefly. Some prophets are used powerfully in the gift of healing, and see or hear in visual or audio form, the names and location and dates of diseases, tumors, injuries, etc. in human bodies. Other prophets include prophetic acts in their words. Prophecies involving national security, bomb threats, terrorist attacks, assassination attempts, etc. require special handling and referral to proper authorities and/or security channels. Other prophecies may have elements of natural disasters, economic calamity, impending judgment, private sin, or a call to repentance or revival. These will typically require special attention, and at times, a public response. Children can prophesy and discern good and evil, angels and spirits, and have spiritual experiences, but are not yet matured fully to judge all aspects of prophecy. Finally, in the mission field or home (cell) group settings when there are no elders or five-fold leaders present, body-level discernment and judging of prophecy is appropriate. The body can still discern in larger corporate settings, but their job then is to share their discernment with leadership.

I hope that this inquiry has been helpful to you in stimulating your thinking and will provide some answers and perhaps provoke and elicit a few questions about this important subject. This concludes our last chapter and we turn now to the Epilogue.

Author's Note: *Prophecies, whether given publicly or privately, should be recorded whenever possible and appropriate for a variety of reasons—teaching, training, accountability, safety, protection, convenience, accuracy, sharing, judging, liability, history, etc.*

Prophetic Lifestyle

Many people, including some Christians — and perhaps especially Christians with the spirit of religion at work in their lives — have a distorted and uninformed view of modern-day prophecy, prophetic ministry and the Prophetic Lifestyle. This book is one step and one tool in changing that. As someone has wisely said, "It is better to light one candle than curse the darkness." Some still use John the Baptist as a role model for prophets today and expect an ascetic from the wilderness wearing camel hair clothing and drinking goat's milk, while others are looking for a generation like Samson who will take a Nazarite vow not to cut their hair or drink wine. In other words, many in the church expect modern-day prophets to be weird, different, odd, unusual, abnormal, isolated, out of touch with "reality," and living on the edge or the fringe of society and mainstream thought and culture.

As a result of these false expectations and outdated mental models, prophets and prophetic ministry have tended to be misunderstood, stereotyped, devalued, distrusted, disrespected and dishonored by the mainstream church. Nothing could be further from God's design and plan for prophecy and prophets today and throughout history. God is looking for more than a prophetic spirit, gift, mantle, unction or function; He is looking for a Prophetic Lifestyle. God is looking for relevant and credible spokespersons, diplomats, stewards and ambassadors to represent Him, His Kingdom and His Word in the earth realm. Most of these people are already in position and functioning in leadership roles in the marketplace and government rather than the "prophetic conference circuit" or the ecclesiastical realm, but have not yet been recognized or activated in some cases or released into the fullness and convergence of their callings in other cases.

> God has need of mature, wise and seasoned prophets in His service.

As such, they represent the modern-day Josephs, Daniels, Esthers, Mordecais, Nehemiahs, Lydias and Corneliuses, not to mention Cyruses, who have been born and raised up for such a time as this. Some of these have been called to be overt and some covert in their functioning and influence. This book is written for you. And just as Jesus is returning for a pure and unspotted bride, God has need of mature, wise and seasoned prophets in His service. This volume is intended as a reference guide and handbook and training manual for those with strategic assignments and prophetic destinies. May you join the ranks of those who have done and are doing mighty exploits for God and His Kingdom, and become part of a prophetic generation. Selah.

Study Guide

In order to fully capture information, it is important to engage your mind beyond simply reading material. Understanding comes as we put theories into practical application. Expertise comes as we gain experience through our application. Use the questions in this study guide to provoke your thoughts and stir your spirit. Allow the questions to stimulate conversations with God and with others. As you think and pray about the material, allow the Holy Spirit to take it to a deeper level and increase your understanding of the prophetic.

Chapter One
Prophetic Style and Voice

1. God is all-powerful. So, why does God use prophecy, i.e., why does He speak through people?

2. How do you find or develop your own prophetic voice and style?

3. God is looking for unique trusted voices. Think about how God speaks to and through you. What are some examples of this?

Chapter Two
Prophecy is Foundational, Not Optional

1. Why do some Christians believe that prophecy is optional? What does Scripture say about that?

2. Is it okay to obey in hopes of receiving the specific rewards mentioned in 2 Chronicles 20:20 and Matthew 10:41? In other words, does God honor us any more or any less if we obey Him in hopes of getting something in return? Consider Romans 8:28 and Jeremiah 29:11 when answering this question.

3. How does being well-versed in Scripture help you in the practice of partnering with the prophetic?

4. How can you learn to hear God's voice?

5. Why is the prophetic central to the mission of the Church?

Chapter Three
Prophetic Protocols

1. Are you submitted to spiritual authority? If not, how can God trust you with authority in prophetic ministry? If yes, have you observed God promoting you as you are faithful to serve someone else?

2. What are the benefits of writing down or recording the prophecies that you give and receive?

3. What are your duties regarding the prophecy once you have given it to someone?

4. What is the difference between ministering on your own and ministering with a team?

5. Who is authorized to prophesy concerning dates, mates, and weights—directional prophecy?

6. What is prophetic drama?

Chapter Four
Prophetic Processes

1. What are the two most common mistakes people make concerning prophecy?

2. What does Scripture say about prophetic timetables?

3. In what ways is presumption a hindrance to prophecy?

4. Why are prophetic confirmation and establishment important?

5. What happens when people try to promote themselves ahead of God's plan for them?

Prophetic Strategy

1. Discuss the role wisdom plays in relationship to prophetic strategy.

2. If God gives you a very clear, direct strategic input, and you ignore it, what might be the consequences?

3. Cite some examples in Scripture where God gave prophetic strategy to His servants.

Prophetic Intercession

1. What is intercession and how does it relate to the prophetic?

2. Discuss the importance of wisdom and discretion regarding things God reveals to you in the spirit realm.

3. Do you have an intercession team for your business or ministry? If yes, how is it working for you? If no, how do you go about building one?

Chapter Seven

Prophetic Activation

1. List specific instances when you received a prophetic word that impacted or resonated with your spirit. How did you feel when this happened? What did it release in you?

2. What does it mean for a prophecy or a Scripture to become a **Rhema** word?

3. Think about the creative aspect of prophetic activation. In what ways have you witnessed or experienced this?

Chapter Eight
Prophetic Portfolios

1. What is a prophetic portfolio?

2. What does your prophetic portfolio look like? (Understand that this may develop and shift over time.)

3. What spiritual assets or areas of authority would you like for God to add to your prophetic portfolio?

Chapter Nine
Prophetic Testing

1. Prophetic words often require a process to fulfillment. What is the purpose of this period of testing? How does it prepare you to enter the plans of God for your life?

2. In what areas of your life do you feel ready for God to use you, but God has not yet "put you into the game"?

3. What are possible reasons that God has not yet "taken you off the bench" and released you?

4. How long does this process of Prophetic Testing last in a person's life? Name or list a few examples from Scripture.

Chapter Ten
Prophetic Patterns

1. The author's academic training in leadership, theory construction and leadership, theory construction and finance gave him a strong frame of reference for understanding prophecy and the prophetic. What things in your background provide similar frameworks for you to steward prophetic grace?

2. When you look at the bigger picture of your life, what themes and patterns begin to emerge? What connections and threads seem to appear over and over again?

3. Can you see, appreciate and understand the prophetic tapestry that God is weaving in your life?

Chapter Eleven
Seven Dimensions or Levels of the Prophetic

1. List the seven levels of the prophetic. For each level, give a very brief description of your understanding of what it means.

2. On which level or dimension of the prophetic are you? How do you know?

3. What is the difference between prophetic gift, prophetic spirit, prophetic mantle, prophetic unction and prophetic function?

Chapter Twelve
Twelve Classes or Types of Prophecy

1. List the twelve classes of prophecy.

2. Has the Lord given you any conditional prophecies, as He did with the rich young ruler?

3. What are those conditions, and what more could you be doing for the Kingdom if you met them?

4. In what areas of your life is the enemy introducing counterfeit prophecies?

5. What Kingdom resources are you accessing for help?

Chapter Thirteen
Prophetic Creativity

1. In what areas of your life is God calling you to go beyond your natural talents in partnering with the prophetic?

2. What are some examples of prophetic creativity that you are aware of?

3. What is the difference between creativity and ability? How does God use these together?

4. What does it mean to co-create with God? How is this different from co-laboring with God?

5. Name three examples of prophetic creativity at work.

Chapter Fourteen
Prophetic Perversion

1. Where are you encountering people who are perverting prophecy? What is God telling you to do in response?

2. What are the possible motives and weaknesses of people who pervert the prophetic?

3. Look carefully at your own life to see if any of these areas might be a potential weakness for you. How can you avoid this?

4. What are the outcomes and consequences for those who pervert God's prophetic gift or office?

Chapter Fifteen
Prophetic Promises

1. Name an example of a prophetic promise in Scripture.

2. Name a prophetic promise that you have received.

3. Why are prophetic promises important?

4. How long does it take for prophetic promises to be fulfilled and come to pass?

Chapter Sixteen
Prophetic Partnership

1. What is keeping you from partnering with the prophetic?

2. What will you do to remove those impediments?

3. How should the five-fold gifts interact and interrelate with each other? Where does prophecy fit in?

4. What does it mean for prophecy to be part of the foundational structure and gift mix of the church?

Chapter Seventeen
Judging Prophecy

1. What does it mean to judge prophecy?

2. Who is authorized and instructed to judge prophecy?

3. What are the 9 steps in judging prophecy?

Epilogue
Prophetic Lifestyle

1. What does it mean to lead or live a prophetic lifestyle?

2. Why are prophecy and prophets a central and important part of God's eternal plan for His church and Kingdom?

3. Why is it important for prophecy to become a daily part of our Christian walk and witness, and to be shared with others outside of the church in the Seven Mountains or Spheres of Cultural Influence?

If any man speak,
let him speak as the
oracles of God; if any
man minister, let him
do it as of the ability
which God giveth: that
God in all things may be
glorified through Jesus
Christ, to whom be
praise and dominion for
ever and ever. Amen.

1 Peter 4:11 KJV

About the Author

Biographical Sketch for Dr. Bruce Cook

Bruce Cook, Ph.D., has significant experience in business consulting, fundraising, private equity investments, business development, marketing, corporate communications, research and higher education and is considered a leading authority on private equity, fundraising and philanthropy. He is a frequent speaker for conferences, seminars and workshops, resides in the Lakebay, Washington area, and is married with two grown sons and a grand-daughter. Currently he is a speaker, author, publisher, convener, network leader, financial consultant and business advisor as well as the President and Founder of VentureAdvisers, Inc., Kingdom Economic Yearly Summit (KEYS), Kingdom House Publishing, Keys Network and Glory Realm Ministries. In addition, he is a director or trustee of WorkLife, Gig Harbor Family Church, The Glory House Ministries, Keys Network, Kingdom Regency Alliance, First State Manufacturing, and Indigenous People's Foundation. Earlier Cook was Research Coordinator for the University of Texas Investment Management Company (UTIMCO), where he was a member of the Private Markets team responsible for alternative asset investments totaling $500 million per year. Prior to that he was Assistant Manager of the largest bank in Arkansas, Worthen Bank, now owned by Bank of America. Dr. Cook is an author, ordained minister, conference and seminar speaker, and contemporary Christian songwriter and producer. His CD's include *Songs in the Night* (2003), *Daddy's in the House* (2004) and *Wealth of the Kingdom* (co-producer, 2008); *Seven Mountain Symphony: Transforming the 7 Mountains of Culture* was released in Feb. 2009 (co-producer). He also served as General Editor of *Aligning with the Apostolic: An Anthology of Apostleship, Vols. 1-5* (2013). Bruce is a spiritual father to many sons and daughters in the marketplace.

To Contact the Author:

To contact the author for speaking engagements— conferences, churches, and motivational events, or strategic business and financial consulting:

wbcook@centurylink.net
brucecook77@gmail.com

For More Information Visit:

www.keysnetwork.org
www.kingdomhouse.net
www.ventureadvisers.com
www.kingdomeconomicsummit.com
www.kingdomventures.com
www.sozolife.com/brucecook
www.gloryrealm.net
www.solavei.com/brucecook
www.gigharborfamilychurch.org

Key Scriptures Relating to Prophecy

I have compiled a list of some key Scriptures relating to prophecy. This list is by no means exhaustive, but will give you some references to further your study of the prophetic. In many cases, I have included more than one translation of the same passage. When I study the Word, I find that reading from many translations brings clarity, richness, and greater understanding. I encourage you to meditate on these Scriptures and allow the Holy Spirit to bring illumination.

1 Samuel 3:19-21 *(New International Version)*_____

> *The LORD was with Samuel as he grew up, and he
> let none of Samuel's words fall to the ground. And all
> Israel from Dan to Beersheba recognized that Samuel
> was attested as a prophet of the LORD. The LORD
> continued to appear at Shiloh, and there he revealed
> himself to Samuel through his word.*

1 Samuel 3:19-21 *(The Message)*_____

Samuel grew up. GOD was with him, and Samuel's prophetic record was flawless. Everyone in Israel, from Dan in the north to Beersheba in the south, recognized that Samuel was the real thing—a true prophet of GOD. GOD continued to show up at Shiloh, revealed through his word to Samuel at Shiloh.

1 Samuel 3:19-21 *(Amplified Bible)*_____

Samuel grew; the Lord was with him and let none of his words fall to the ground.

And all Israel from Dan to Beersheba knew that Samuel was established to be a prophet of the Lord.

And the Lord continued to appear in Shiloh, for the Lord revealed Himself to Samuel in Shiloh through the word of the Lord.

1 Samuel 3:19-21 *(King James Version)*_____

And Samuel grew, and the LORD was with him, and did let none of his words fall to the ground.

And all Israel from Dan even to Beersheba knew that Samuel was established to be a prophet of the LORD.

And the LORD appeared again in Shiloh: for the LORD revealed himself to Samuel in Shiloh by the word of the LORD.

2 Chronicles 20:20 *(Amplified Bible—Emphasis Added)*_____

And they rose early in the morning and went out into the Wilderness of Tekoa; and as they went out, Jehoshaphat stood and said, Hear me, O Judah, and you inhabitants of Jerusalem! **Believe** *in the Lord your God and you* **shall** *be established;* **believe** *and remain steadfast to* **His prophets** *and you* **shall prosper.**

2 Chronicles 20:20 *(King James Version)*_____

And they rose early in the morning, and went forth into the wilderness of Tekoa: and as they went forth, Jehoshaphat stood and said, Hear me, O Judah, and ye inhabitants of Jerusalem; Believe in the LORD your God, so shall ye be established; believe his prophets, so shall ye prosper.

Amos 3:7 *(Amplified Bible)*_____

Surely the Lord God will do nothing without revealing His secret to His servants the prophets.

Amos 3:7 *(New International Version)*_____

Surely the Sovereign LORD does nothing without revealing his plan to his servants the prophets.

Amos 3:7 *(The Message)*_____

The fact is, God, the Master, does nothing without first telling his prophets the whole story.

Matthew 10:41 *(Amplified Bible)*_____

He who receives and welcomes and accepts a prophet because he is a prophet shall receive a prophet's reward, and he who receives and welcomes and accepts a righteous man because he is a righteous man shall receive a righteous man's reward.

Matthew 10:41 *(New International Version)*_____

Whoever welcomes a prophet as a prophet will receive a prophet's reward, and whoever welcomes a righteous person as a righteous person will receive a righteous person's reward.

Matthew 10:41 *(King James Version)*_____

He that receiveth a prophet in the name of a prophet shall receive a prophet's reward; and he that receiveth a righteous man in the name of a righteous man shall receive a righteous man's reward.

Matthew 10:41 *(The Message)*_____

Accepting a messenger of God is as good as being God's messenger. Accepting someone's help is as good as giving someone help.

1 Corinthians 12:28 *(New International Version)*_____

And God has placed in the church first of all apostles, second prophets, third teachers, then miracles, then gifts of healing, of helping, of guidance, and of different kinds of tongues.

1 Corinthians 12:28 *(The Message)*_____

You are Christ's body—that's who you are! You must never forget this. Only as you accept your part of that body does your "part" mean anything. You're familiar with some of the parts that God has formed in his church, which is his "body": apostles, prophets, teachers, miracle workers, healers, helpers, organizers, those who pray in tongues. But it's obvious by now, isn't it, that Christ's church is a complete Body and not a gigantic, unidimensional Part? It's not all Apostle, not all Prophet, not all Miracle Worker, not all Healer, not all Prayer in Tongues, not all Interpreter of Tongues. And yet some of you keep competing for so-called "important" parts. But now I want to lay out a far better way for you.

1 Corinthians 12:28 *(Amplified Bible)*_____

So God has appointed some in the church [for His own use]: first apostles (special messengers); second prophets (inspired preachers and expounders); third teachers; then wonder-workers; then those with ability to heal the sick; helpers; administrators; [speakers in] different (unknown) tongues.

1 Corinthians 12:28 *(King James Version)*_____

And God hath set some in the church, first apostles, secondarily prophets, thirdly teachers, after that miracles, then gifts of healings, helps, governments, diversities of tongues.

1 Corinthians 13:8-10 (King James Version)_____

Charity never faileth: but whether there be prophecies, they shall fail; whether there be tongues, they shall cease; whether there be knowledge, it shall vanish away.

For we know in part, and we prophesy in part. But when that which is perfect is come, then that which is in part shall be done away.

1 Corinthians 13:8-10 (Amplified Bible)_____

Love never fails [never fades out or becomes obsolete or comes to an end]. As for prophecy (the gift of interpreting the divine will and purpose), it will be fulfilled and pass away; as for tongues, they will be destroyed and cease; as for knowledge, it will pass away [it will lose its value and be superseded by truth].

For our knowledge is fragmentary (incomplete and imperfect), and our prophecy (our teaching) is fragmentary (incomplete and imperfect).

But when the complete and perfect (total) comes, the incomplete and imperfect will vanish away (become antiquated, void, and superseded).

1 Corinthians 13:8-10 (The Message)_____

Love never dies. Inspired speech will be over some day; praying in tongues will end; understanding will reach its limit. We know only a portion of the truth, and what we say about God is always incomplete. But when the Complete arrives, our incompletes will be canceled.

Corinthians 13:8-10 (New International Version)_____

Love never fails. But where there are prophecies, they will cease; where there are tongues, they will be stilled; where there is knowledge, it will pass away. [9] For we know in part and we prophesy in part, [10] but when completeness comes, what is in part disappears.

Corinthians 14:1 (Amplified Bible—Emphais Added)_____

EAGERLY PURSUE and seek to acquire [this] love [make it your aim, your great quest]; and earnestly desire and **cultivate** *the spiritual endowments (gifts), especially that you may prophesy (interpret the divine will and purpose in inspired preaching and teaching).*

Note: See for reference Heb. 5:14 NIV "But solid food is for the mature, who **by constant use have trained themselves** to distinguish good from evil.

Corinthians 14:1 (New International Version—Emphasis Added)_____

Follow the way of love and eagerly desire gifts of the Spirit, especially **prophecy***.*

Corinthians 14:3 (King James Version)_____

But he that prophesieth speaketh unto men to edification, and exhortation, and comfort.

1 Corinthians 14:3 *(Amplified Bible)*_____

But [on the other hand], the one who prophesies [who interprets the divine will and purpose in inspired preaching and teaching] speaks to men for their upbuilding and constructive spiritual progress and encouragement and consolation.

1 Corinthians 14:3 *(New International Version)*_____

But the one who prophesies speaks to people for their strengthening, encouraging and comfort.

1 Corinthians 14:22 *(New International Version—Emphasis Added)*_____

Tongues, then, are a sign, not for believers but for unbelievers; **prophecy***, however, is not for unbelievers but for believers.*

.

1 Corinthians 14:29 *(New International Version)*_____

Two or three prophets should speak, and the others should weigh carefully what is said.

1 Corinthians 14:29 *(Amplified Bible)*_____

So let two or three prophets speak [those inspired to preach or teach], while the rest pay attention and weigh and discern what is said.

1 Corinthians 14:31 *(New International Version)*_____

For you can all prophesy in turn so that everyone may be instructed and encouraged.

1 Corinthians 14:31 *(King James Version)*_____

For ye may all prophesy one by one, that all may learn, and all may be comforted.

1 Corinthians 14:31 *(Amplified Bible)*_____

For in this way you can give testimony [prophesying and thus interpreting the divine will and purpose] one by one, so that all may be instructed and all may be stimulated and encouraged;

Ephesians 2:19-20 *(New International Version)*_____

Consequently, you are no longer foreigners and strangers, but fellow citizens with God's people and also members of his household, built on the foundation of the apostles and prophets, with Christ Jesus himself as the chief cornerstone.

Ephesians 2:19-20 *(The Message)*_____

That's plain enough, isn't it? You're no longer wandering exiles. This kingdom of faith is now your home country. You're no longer strangers or outsiders. You belong here, with as much right to the name Christian as anyone. God is building a home. He's using us all—irrespective of how we got here—in what he is building. He used the apostles and prophets for the foundation. Now he's using you, fitting you in brick by brick, stone by stone, with Christ Jesus as the cornerstone that holds all the parts together. We see it taking shape day after day—a holy temple built by

God, all of us built into it, a temple in which God is quite at home.

Ephesians 2:19-20 *(Amplified Bible)*_____

Therefore you are no longer outsiders (exiles, migrants, and aliens, excluded from the rights of citizens), but you now share citizenship with the saints (God's own people, consecrated and set apart for Himself); and you belong to God's [own] household. You are built upon the foundation of the apostles and prophets with Christ Jesus Himself the chief Cornerstone.

Ephesians 2:19-20 *(King James Version)*_____

Now therefore ye are no more strangers and foreigners, but fellowcitizens with the saints, and of the household of God; And are built upon the foundation of the apostles and prophets, Jesus Christ himself being the chief corner stone.

Ephesians 4:11 *(New International Version)*_____

So Christ himself gave the apostles, the prophets, the evangelists, the pastors and teachers,

Ephesians 4:11 *(Amplified Bible)*_____

And His gifts were [varied; He Himself appointed and gave men to us] some to be apostles (special messengers), some prophets (inspired preachers and expounders), some evangelists (preachers of the Gospel, traveling missionaries), some pastors (shepherds of His flock) and teachers.

Ephesians 4:11 *(King James Version)*_____

And he gave some, apostles; and some, prophets; and some, evangelists; and some, pastors and teachers;

1 Peter 4:11 *(King James Version)*_____

If any man speak, let him speak as the oracles of God; if any man minister, let him do it as of the ability which God giveth: that God in all things may be glorified through Jesus Christ, to whom be praise and dominion for ever and ever. Amen.

1 Peter 4:11 *(Amplified Bible)*_____

Whoever speaks, [let him do it as one who utters] oracles of God; whoever renders service, [let him do it] as with the strength which God furnishes abundantly, so that in all things God may be glorified through Jesus Christ (the Messiah). To Him be the glory and dominion forever and ever (through endless ages). Amen (so be it).

1 Peter 4:11 *(New International Version)*_____

If anyone speaks, they should do so as one who speaks the very words of God. If anyone serves, they should do so with the strength God provides, so that in all things God may be praised through Jesus Christ. To him be the glory and the power for ever and ever. Amen.

2 Peter 1:19 *(The Message—Emphasis Added)* _____

We couldn't be more sure of what we saw and heard—God's glory, God's voice. The prophetic Word was **confirmed** *to us.*

2 Peter 1:19 *(New International Version)*_____

We also have the prophetic message as something completely reliable, and you will do well to pay attention to it, as to a light shining in a dark place, until the day dawns and the morning star rises in your hearts.

2 Peter 1:21 *(Amplified Bible—Emphasis Added)*_____

For no **prophecy** *ever originated because some man willed it [to do so-it never came by human impulse], but men spoke from God who were* **borne along** *(moved and impelled) by the Holy* **Spirit***.*

2 Peter 1:21 *(King James Version—Emphasis Added)*_____

For the prophecy came not in old time by the will of man: but holy men of God spake as they were **moved** *by the Holy Ghost.*

2 Peter 1:21 *(New International Version—Emphasis Added)*_____

For prophecy never had its origin in the human will, but prophets, though human, spoke from God as they were **carried along** *by the Holy Spirit.*